Clinics in Developmental Medicine No. 23

The Motor Deficit in Patients with Cerebral Palsy

BY

Karel Bobath

PREFACE BY

R. C. Mac Keith

Published by Spastics International Medical Publications in Association with William Heinemann Medical Books Ltd.

SBN 433-03330-4

First published 1966 ; reprinted 1969, 1972, 1974

Printed in England at THE LAVENHAM PRESS LTD., Lavenham, Suffolk.

To my wife

Contents

Preface

Recent years have seen an increasing interest taken in cerebral palsy as well as in other previously neglected chronic illnesses of childhood. The associated increased interest in the whole field of neurological and psychological disorders of childhood has led to closer study of earlier stages of development. Simultaneously paediatrics has advanced into the study of the newborn and of his neurology. These changes and the special interest of paediatrics in prevention are leading to earlier diagnosis and treatment.

To our better understanding of the underlying neuropathophysiology and treatment of cerebral palsy Karel and Berta Bobath have, I believe, made a great contribution, probably the major contribution.

The learning of voluntary movement appears to depend on the achievement of the movement. More fundamentally it is based on the sensation of the movement. This applies in the normal child's learning and in that of the child with a motor handicap. Treatment by physiotherapy includes active and passive movement but only active movement can give the sensations essential for the learning of voluntary movement.

If the motor education of the child with cerebral palsy is postponed to an age at which he can cooperate actively, treatment will be neglected during the earlier years, and he will have, by the time he can participate in his treatment, acquired many disordered patterns. Yet passive movement cannot teach willed movement.

By using the automatic postural responses present from an early age, the Bobaths solved this apparently insoluble problem. The child who is too young to cooperate can still be induced to make active movements. In addition the development of disadvantageous patterns and postures can be diminished, for the Bobaths have shown that much of the disordered posture and movement typical of cerebral palsy are the result of unchecked postural responses either persisting to abnormally late age or abnormal in other ways.

The more recent application of their ideas in the very early treatment of infants under the age of one year, before the disordered postures and movements are established, suggests that in many cases much of the disorder may be prevented — a most exciting possibility.

The validity of treatment methods in cerebral palsy is not easy to establish. But it is at least more inviting to undertake research on methods which appear to have a sound neurophysiological basis.

In this book Dr. Karel Bobath sets out the neurophysiological mechanisms which underlie the motor disorders of cerebral palsy. They also form the logical basis of the techniques of treatment which Mrs. Berta Bobath and he have advocated and which have won world-wide acceptance.

Their teaching has had great influence for good for they have continuously searched for explanation as well as for better techniques. We are happy to be publishing this book which we believe will be of great usefulness to paediatricians, neurologists, and therapists.

R. C. Mac Keith

CHAPTER I

Introduction

Cerebral Palsy is the result of a lesion or maldevelopment of the brain, non-progressive in character and existing from earliest childhood. The motor deficit finds expression in abnormal patterns of posture and movement, in association with an abnormal postural tone. The lesion which is present in the brain when it is still immature interferes with the normal motor development of the child.

Normal Motor Development: General Remarks

Normal motor development proceeds in an orderly sequence of events. For an understanding of the nature of the motor handicap of a child with brain damage it is important to study normal motor development in terms of the evolution of the automatic postural reactions which underlie a child's overt functional activities. These reactions form the background of posture and movement which the child adapts as he learns to perform any skilled activity, like sitting up and remaining sitting, rolling over, standing up, and walking. For this reason such reactions have been called, by Schaltenbrand (1927), 'Principal Motility.'

Essentially, normal motor development is characterised by two sets of processes which are closely interwoven and dependent upon each other. They are:—

1. The development of a normal postural reflex mechanism which is not present at birth and which in time will become highly complex and varied. Righting, equilibrium and other adaptive and protective reactions fall into this group. The development of these reactions is closely associated with a normal postural tone which allows for the maintenance of positions against gravity and the performance of normal movements.

2. The inhibition of some of the responses of the neonate, a process which may be associated with the maturation of the brain. Examples of this inhibition are primary standing and walking, the startle reaction, and the tonic finger flexion response. It shows itself also in a change of the early total responses, such as the total withdrawal response involving all the segments of a limb, also a change which involves inhibition. This process, sometimes referred to as 'breaking up' of the early total responses, makes possible a re-synthesis of parts of the total patterns in many and varied ways, and, in association with the development of a normal postural reflex mechanism referred to in (1), allows for the performance of selective movements such as walking and especially for the perfection of manipulative skills. It is likely that the nerve pathways used in the neonate are still available under certain conditions of facilitation. It has for example been shown that primary walking, which is usually considered to be inhibited from the age of 2 or 3 months, can, in fact, be evoked throughout the first year by passive extension of the head (Mac Keith 1964), and the automatic

1

patterns of motor co-ordination involved are probably available for use under voluntary control in the definitive walking which emerges at 12 or 13 months.

An important feature of normal motor development (as we shall see) is the freeing of arms and hands from their early role of supporting posture and balance. In time this function is relegated to trunk and legs.

Motor Development in Cerebral Palsy: General Remarks

In cerebral palsy the lesion interferes with this orderly development. Essentially, this will result in a retardation or arrest of development with:—

1. An insufficiently developed postural reflex mechanism, showing itself, for instance, in poor head control, lack of rotation within the body axis, and lack of balance and other adaptive reactions.

2. A lack of inhibition showing itself in unduly prolonged retention of the primitive total patterns of earliest childhood.

During the first few months, this retardation of motor development may be the only feature of cerebral damage. This is especially so in the milder cases and also in those babies in whom the lower limbs are predominantly affected. Here the differentiation of cerebral palsy from the motor retardation of mental retardation or subnormality may be very difficult. However, in cerebral palsy signs of abnormal postural activity, that is, of a release of the tonic reflexes of Magnus (1924, 1926) and Walshe (1923), will make their appearance sooner or later, depending on the severity of the case. They will produce abnormal postures and movements with well-defined patterns of co-ordination which are incompatible with normal motor activity.

For an early recognition of cases of cerebral palsy it is, therefore, important to discriminate as soon as possible between primitive responses which are normal but present at an abnormal age, and motor behaviour which is abnormal.

Motor behaviour may be defined as *primitive* if the patterns of posture and movement are those which are normally seen at some stage of a normal full-term baby's post-natal life but in time disappear or become modified. Examples are the Moro reflex, the primitive so-called 'grasp reflex', crossed extension kicking, the neck righting reaction and the asymmetrical tonic neck response.

Motor behaviour may be defined as *abnormal* if the patterns of posture and movement observed, such as, for instance, tonic reflexes producing abnormal postural tone, do not correspond to those found at any time during a normal baby's post-natal life. (For a description of these abnormal postural reflexes see page 13).

To understand and interpret correctly the nature of the motor deficit of children with cerebral palsy it is, therefore, necessary to have a good working knowledge of normal child development. It is necessary to be able to interpret the child's overt functional behaviour (as described by Gesell and Amatruda (1947), Illingworth (1960), Schaltenbrand (1927) and others), in terms of both the evolution of normal postural reflex mechanisms and the elaboration of early total patterns of motor co-ordination. One will also have to study the various abnormal postural reflexes, their specific patterns of co-ordination, the way in which they differ from normal primitive patterns and the manner in which they interfere with normal motor activity.

CHAPTER II

Normal Motor Development: Special Features

1. The Neo-Natal Period

This chapter is not a full account of normal motor development but, rather, describes certain aspects of this development which are of particular significance in the study of children who may have cerebral palsy. Generally speaking, the newborn full-term baby shows at rest a symmetrical attitude of flexion in all positions, whether supine, prone, vertical or in ventral suspension (Fig. 1 *a*, *b*, *c*). This is due to a physiological flexor hypertonus of the muscles of trunk and limbs which is of a symmetrical distribution. The limbs will resist passive extension. Head control is poor.

The arms are fairly firmly fixed to the trunk in an attitude of flexion. The hands are fisted, and the thumb adducted. (The fingers, as André-Thomas and Saint-Anne Dargassies (1960) rightly stress, do not show a true grasp reflex, but a tonic reaction of the finger flexors, a proprioceptive response to stretch of these muscles.) Though the arms and hands will resist passive extension, they will nevertheless extend reflexly in the Moro reflex (startle reaction), which at this stage consists of a wide abduction of the arms, extension at the elbows and wrists, and extension with abduction of thumbs and fingers. (First phase of the startle reaction, Fig. 2.)

The lower limbs are more mobile and show alternating flexion and extension (crossed extension kicking) both in the supine and prone positions. These movements are distinct from the flexion and crossed extension reflexes seen in spinal animals (Fulton 1951), in that the hips do not fully extend in kicking, and although the legs may adduct slightly with extension, they retain their outward rotation and the ankles remain dorsiflexed.

Of all the righting reactions only the neck righting reaction is present. Active or passive turning of the baby's head to one side will be followed by rotation of the spine which, if the reaction is strong enough, will make the baby turn to that side, the trunk following the head (Fig. 3). The labyrinthine righting reaction on the head is still very weak and it is probably for this reason that the baby has poor control. In the prone position, he cannot raise his head for more than a moment, although he will turn his head to one side (Illingworth 1960). Optical righting reactions are not yet present.

Equilibrium reactions are absent. If the baby is placed in the supine or prone position on a table which is then tilted to one side, he will roll over towards the lower side without any adaptive reaction (Weisz 1938).

The asymmetrical tonic neck response is not conspicuous in the newborn. The position of the arms is rarely affected by spontaneous or passive rotation of the head. The newborn is flexed and symmetrical, and more definite asymmetrical tonic-neck-attitudes will only appear towards the forth or fifth week when the baby has developed more extensor tone. Even then, this response is very unpredictable and variable and not sufficiently strong to interfere with the baby's general activities. A study of 108 healthy newborn babies between the first and sixth day by Karlsson and Vassella

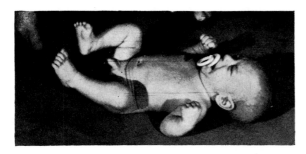

Fig. 1a. Normal child in supine position. Predominant flexion.

Fig. 1b. Normal child in prone position. Predominant flexion, head turned to one side.

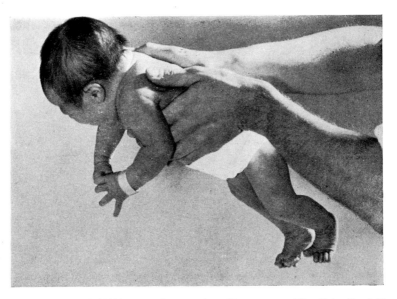

Fig. 1c. Normal child in ventral suspension. (*By courtesy of Dr. Heinz Prechtl.*)

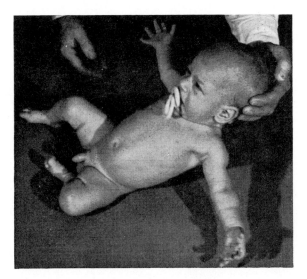

Fig. 2. First phase of the startle reaction.

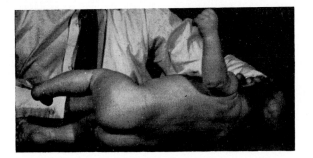

Fig. 3. The neck righting reaction. Head rotation is followed by rotation of the body as a whole. Normal baby 8 weeks old.

(1962) has shown that in only nine of them (8 per cent) could the asymmetrical tonic neck response be observed with the regularity of a true reflex.

Other Automatic Reactions

In the newborn these include primary standing, early automatic walking, Galant's reaction (the incurvation of the trunk) and the placing reaction of the legs.

(1) *Primary standing* is obtained by placing the baby with his feet on a table. He will then gradually right himself and assume the standing position*. This righting ability gradually disappears during the second month (André-Thomas *et al.* 1952, 1960). According to Peiper (1961) the assumption of the 'primary' standing posture in the neonate is the result of the positive supporting reaction of the legs.

*Fig 6*b*, showing the placing reaction, illustrates this.

5

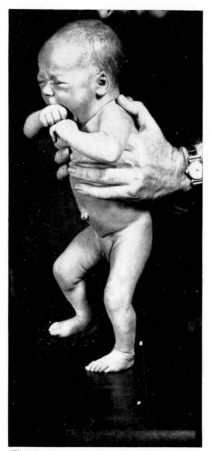

Fig. 4. Automatic walking. (*By courtesy of Prof. R. S. Paine.*)

(2) *Automatic walking* can be elicited by placing the baby with his feet on a table while the examiner supports the baby's trunk with both hands. The legs will extend and the baby will right himself to assume the standing position. If the body in righting is now tilted slightly forward the baby will begin to walk with well coordinated and rhythmical steps (Fig. 4). His hips and knees are, however, never fully extended. The equilibrium functions of the trunk and co-contraction of the muscles of the trunk necessary for maintaining the upright position are absent and if support is withdrawn the baby will collapse. This walking persists for a variable period of up to two months (André-Thomas *et al.* 1960). However, according to Mac Keith (1964) primary walking can still be obtained in most babies under one year of age by combining the above-described manoeuvre with passive extension of the baby's head.

(3) *Galant's reaction* (the trunk incurvation reflex) is tested with the baby prone or in ventral suspension. The skin of the lumbar region between the twelfth rib and the iliac crest is pricked lightly and repeatedly. This will result in a lateral flexion of the trunk toward the stimulated side (Fig. 5). According to André-Thomas *et al.* (1960) this reaction will normally disappear during the second month. Ingram (1962) has observed it in babies up to three months. (In a child with cerebral palsy, especially of the athetoid group, the reaction may, however, persist for much longer. Its retention may cause considerable delay in the development of symmetrical stabilization of the trunk and of independent movements of the head which are necessary for sitting, standing and walking.) This instability of the trunk seems to be further aggravated by the persistence of an asymmetrical tonic neck reflex.

(4) *The placing reaction of the legs* is obtained by lifting the baby into the upright position and gently bringing the anterior aspect of the leg or the dorsum of the foot into contact with the edge of the table. The baby will flex the leg and bring the foot above the surface of the table. This will be followed by extension of the legs so that the sole of the foot touches the surface (Fig. 6 *a* and *b*). According to André-Thomas *et al.* (1960) this reaction is obtainable after the first ten days. Prechtl and Beintema (1964) also found that the reaction was not pronounced during the first four days.

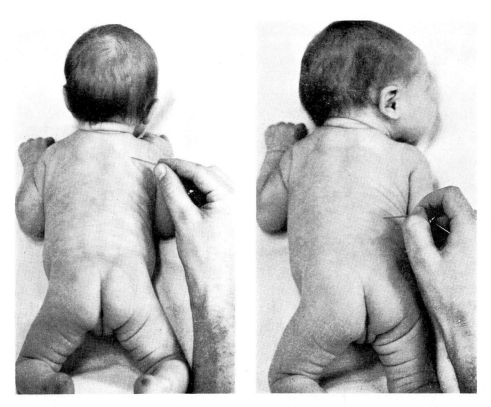

Fig. 5. Incurvation of the trunk (Galant's reaction). (*a*) Stimulation. (*b*) Response. (*By courtesy of Dr. Heinz Prechtl.*)

The statement that the absence of the placing reaction is closely associated with a severe degree of mental subnormality (Zappella *et al*. 1964) must be accepted with great reservation. It has been found to be absent also in children with severe degrees of extensor spasticity of the legs, regardless of the degree of mental retardation.

An important feature of the motor behaviour of normal babies is its *variability*. None of the various responses and reactions above described can be obtained always or with regularity. This variable and unpredictable nature of the responses to adequate stimulation points to the influence of *higher centres* on the early automatic reactions and argues against the statement that the newborn is a 'pallidum being' (Peiper 1961).

2. The Next Ten Months

Gradually the normal automatic reactions for the maintenance of posture and equilibrium develop. First come the remaining righting reactions. They originate in the labyrinths, in the proprioceptors of the neck muscles (and probably of the ligaments of the cervical spine), in the touch and pressure receptors of trunk and limbs, and in the eyes.

The function of the righting reactions is the maintenance of the normal position of the head in space and the proper alignment of head and neck with the trunk, and

7

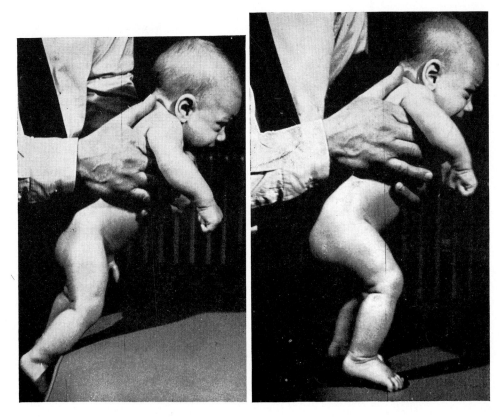

Fig. 6a.   Fig. 6b.

Fig. 6 a, b.   Placing reactions of the legs. Normal baby 8 weeks old.

of the trunk with the limbs. Righting by vision, that is, through the optical righting reactions, eventually becomes predominant, but it is not known when this happens. This process probably begins around the sixth month, that is, at a time when the normal head position and its alignment with the trunk has been fairly well established with the help of the labyrinthine and body righting reaction on the head.

The baby gradually improves the control of his head. The labyrinthine righting reaction on the head allows first for the raising of the head in the prone position. At first the head can be held up only weakly and intermittently, but the baby can do this fairly well in midline from about the eighth week. This improving head control can also be seen when the baby is pulled to sitting from supine lying. Although at first he is not able to raise his head and to assist in this way when pulled up to sitting, his head will begin to move forward at about three months of age and from the fourth month on there will be only a slight initial head lag (Fig. 7). From the sixth month on only a slight initial pull on the arms is required to assist him in sitting up.

Head raising in the prone position initiates a process of general extension of trunk and limbs against gravity which proceeds cephalo-caudad to reach hips and knees around the sixth month (Fig. 8). By this time, the normal baby is also able to raise

8

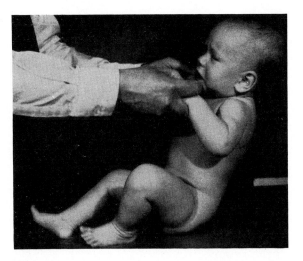

Fig. 7. Normal child of 5 months pulled to sitting. The head is well aligned with the trunk; the hips and knees are still flexed.

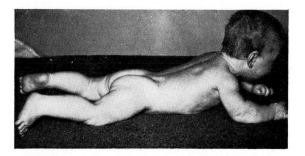

Fig. 8. Normal baby at 6 months. Extension has reached hips and knees.

his head against gravity by flexing it forward from supine lying. Up to about the fifth to sixth month the normal baby moves with patterns of total flexion or extension against gravity. Therefore, until he is about six months old he is not able to sit with flexed hips and extended legs. There is also a short phase when the prone baby is able to extend his spine, hips and legs fully and to support his weight on extended arms. He is, however, still unable to move into kneeling on all fours; that is, he cannot maintain extension of spine and arms, when attempting to bear his weight on flexed knees. During the next few months both the total extension and flexion patterns are gradually broken up, so that the baby can crawl, kneel, and sit with flexed hips and extended spine and legs. The ability to raise the head in prone lying can thus be seen to be an important factor in ushering in extension of the baby against gravity. Furthermore, head control in the supine and prone positions remains throughout life an important factor of our ability to get up to sitting and standing—actions which are normally initiated by raising the head against gravity.

9

Further righting reactions develop around the sixth to seventh month. The body righting reaction acting on the body breaks up the total rotation pattern of the earlier and more primitive neck righting reaction, in which turning of the head to one side may be followed by a rotation of the body as a whole. It introduces instead rotation within the body axis, the shoulders starting the movement and the hips following, or vice-versa. This, together with the necessary extension of head and trunk, which is established at this stage, allows the baby to turn from supine to prone-lying, and at about eight months to sit up from prone. The body righting reaction acting on the head appears at the same time and enables the baby to right his head in response to information through touch and pressure from body and limbs. It supports and reinforces the labyrinthine righting reaction acting on the head.

Equilibrium reactions appear around the sixth month, first in prone and supine lying, later in sitting, kneeling and standing. They thus follow and partially overlap in time with the developing righting reactions. They are of a more complex nature than the righting reactions. They may be either compensatory movements or invisible shifts of muscle tone throughout the body musculature, which latter can be observed by palpation or E.M.G. studies (Clemessen 1951). They occur automatically and render equilibrium in all positions possible (Fig. 9 *a-g*). They have been studied by Weisz (1938), André-Thomas (1940), Rademaker (1935) and Zador (1938). It is interesting to note that the first equilibrium reactions appear at a time (six months) when the baby already sits, in sitting they only appear when the baby begins to stand, and in standing when the baby begins to walk. This shows the considerable overlap in the development of the basic functional activities in a growing baby, a fact that has to be kept in mind when treating children with cerebral palsy. Equilibrium reactions are gradually perfected over the next five years.

During the second to third month the Moro reflex becomes modified and less brisk. While the arms still abduct at the shoulder, the elbows and fingers do not fully extend. It disappears when the child is able to sit momentarily without support (Ingram 1962). The disappearance of the startle reaction seems to coincide with the appearance of the Landau reaction and of the protective extension of the arms.

The Landau reaction makes its appearance at six months of age. It is observed when the baby is held in ventral suspension supported by one hand under the lower chest. The baby will first right his head; this is followed by symmetrical extension of the thighs at the hips (first phase of the Landau, Fig. 10 *a*). If the head is passively flexed, the thighs will flex also (second phase, Fig. 10 *b*). This symmetrical extension of the trunk and of the thighs at this stage seems to be an important phase towards the development of the standing posture. When the Landau attains its full strength around the eighth month, reciprocal kicking stops (Illingworth 1960).

The protective extension of the arms (propping reaction, André-Thomas *et al.* 1960) appears around the sixth month (Fig. 11). The baby in sitting can support his weight on arms that are extended forward at the sixth month, sideways at the eighth month, and backwards between the tenth and twelfth. At first weight is taken on the fisted hand, although the hands may be open until they touch the support. Soon afterwards, however, the hands will remain open on the supporting surface. This reaction can also be tested by lowering the child from the Landau test position, head first, down

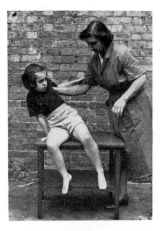

Fig. 9a

Fig. 9b

Fig. 9c

Fig. 9d

Fig. 9e

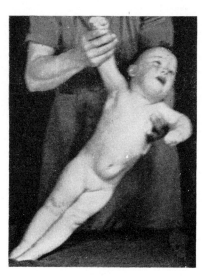

Fig. 9f

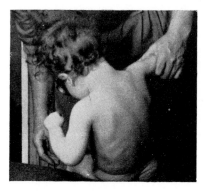

Fig. 9g

Figs. 9a-d.   Normal equilibrium reactions.

Fig. 9e.   Spastic hemiplegia. Spasticity of left leg prevents normal reaction to weight transfer of body backwards.

Fig. 9f.   Spastic quadriplegia; lack of head righting and equilibrium in standing.

Fig. 9g.   Spastic quadriplegia; lack of equilibrium in sitting, and no head righting. Propping reactions of arm prevented by flexor spasticity.

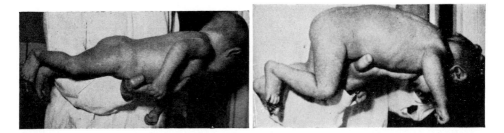

Fig. 10a. Landau reaction, phase 1.　　　**Fig. 10b.** Landau reaction, phase 2.

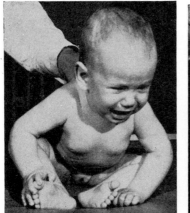

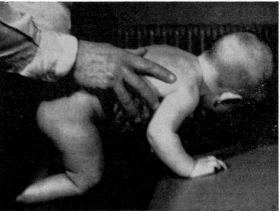

Fig. 11. Normal baby 5 months old, sitting with primitive flexion pattern. Protective extension of the arms (propping reaction) forward is beginning, but still with flexed fingers.

Fig. 12. Normal baby 5 months old. Placing reaction of the arms.

to the support where he will take his weight on extended arms. In this form this re-action has also been called 'precipitation reflex' (André-Thomas *et al.* 1952 and 1960).

Placing reactions of the arms appear towards the end of the third month (Fig. 12). They consist of a placing of arm and hand on the surface of a table, after the dorsum of the hand or the forearm has been brought into light contact with the edge of the table.

CHAPTER III

Motor Development in Cerebral Palsy: Special Features

In cerebral palsy, as stressed before, the lesion interferes with this orderly development. Symptoms of motor retardation are followed, sooner or later, by the appearance of abnormal patterns of posture and movement, in association with abnormal postural tone. With the gradual appearance of tonic reflex activity, extensor and flexor activity become stronger in the supine and prone positions respectively. The cerebral palsied baby, generally speaking, therefore does not develop postural tone against gravity as does the normal child, but he develops abnormal postural reflex activity which will, in fact, cause his body to conform to the pull of gravity. If he is a quadriplegic child and the whole body is involved, he may in time, develop a picture of total extension in supine lying (Fig. 13) and of total flexion in prone lying (Fig.14).

Fig. 13. Total extension picture in supine in a severe case of spastic quadriplegia.

Fig. 14. Spastic quadriplegia: flexor spasticity in prone lying.

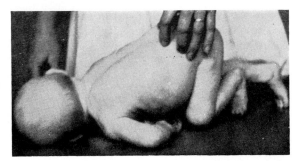

The rate and extent to which this picture develops depends on the type and severity of the case and on how much of the body is involved. Initially, unless the case is a severe one, extensor and flexor hypertonus will show themselves only when the child is handled. For instance, when the baby is pulled up to sitting from supine lying, the

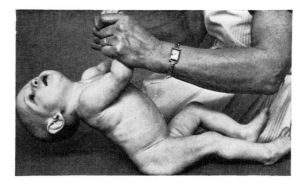

Fig. 15. Head retraction and head lag when pulled to sitting.

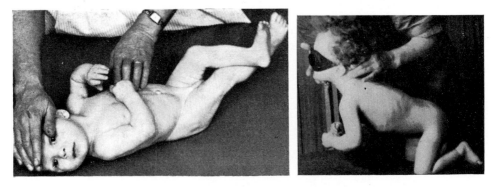

Fig. 16a. Testing for neck righting. Rotation is prevented by retraction of the left shoulder.

Fig. 16b. Tonic labyrinthine reflex: the arms pull up in flexion.

head may lag far behind, neck and shoulders may retract, the hips may resist flexion, and the legs may extend, adduct, and sometimes even cross (Fig. 15). The turning of the head to one side may not be followed by rotation of the trunk (neck righting reaction), as this is prevented by retraction of the shoulders (Fig. 16 a). These may be early signs of a tendency towards excessive extensor activity in the supine position, probably the result of the influence of the tonic labyrinthine reflex. In the prone position, on the other hand, flexor hyperactivity may show itself in the baby's inability to raise his head, in a resistance to passive raising of head and shoulders, and in his inability to extend his arms for support when lifted up by his shoulders (Fig. 16 b), since the propping reaction is prevented by flexor hyperactivity of the arms.

Even in the case of a fully established quadriplegia the clear picture of total extension in supine and of flexion in prone is not the rule. A few of these children, and they are usually the most severe cases, may show in the supine position strong extensor hypertonus with opisthotonus and still show fairly severe extensor hypertonus when lying prone, though less than when lying supine (Fig. 17 a, b). The head may still be retracted in the prone position as long as the child's trunk and legs are stiffly extended. There may then be resistance to passive flexion of the head. However, if one flexes the

14

Fig. 17a.

Fig. 17b.

Fig. 17a, b. Severe spastic quadriplegia: extensor spasticity both in supine and prone with strong retraction of head and neck.

child's thighs at the hips or his legs at the knees, or abducts his thighs, the head will suddenly flex, and he will be unable to raise it. Other cases, a very few in number, may show flexor hypertonus in the prone and supine positions, being very much stronger, however, in the former. In both types of cases one may wonder whether the raised head in the supine or prone positions is the result of normal head righting or of abnormal postural tone. However, the normal baby, from the sixth month on, raises his head in both positions, whereas the severely affected spastic quadriplegic above described does so only in either the prone or supine position. These severe and comparatively rare exceptional cases do not usually offer any difficulty to early diagnosis.

If abnormal postural reflex activity is strong at an early age, or if, as usually happens, it increases during the first years, the child will not acquire many of the abilities of normal children. Hypertonus will develop either in the form of spasticity or rigidity (spastic or plastic hypertonus), or as intermittent increases of postural tone in response to stimulation, so characteristic of the athetoid group of cerebral palsy. Many of the early automatic reactions of movement such as the Moro reflex and crossed

Fig. 18. Retention of startle reaction (spastic quadriplegia with distal athetosis).

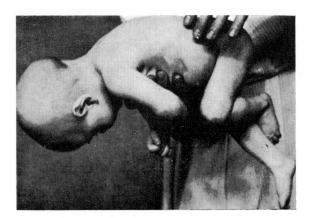

Fig. 19. Spastic quadriplegia: flexor hypertonus preventing Landau reaction.

extension kicking are retained, and righting and equilibrium reactions are absent or insufficiently developed.

The Moro reflex (startle reaction) may remain active long after it should have disappeared, especially in the modified second stage form (Fig. 18). This will interfere with the development of the protective extension reaction of the arms (propping reaction, or precipitation reflex) and make the maintenance of equilibrium in sitting difficult or impossible. The child will also be unable to use his arms for support, for instance, when trying to sit up. The appearance of the propping reaction seems normally to coincide with the disappearance of the Moro reflex.

Flexor spasticity in the prone position will prevent the development of the Landau reaction. This is, therefore, usually absent in children with cerebral palsy (Fig. 19). Occasionally, however, it can be seen prematurely in some of the very severe cases described above, which show strong extensor spasticity with opisthotonus even in prone lying.

Abnormal tonic reflex activity will also interfere with the development of the body righting reaction on the body. Insufficient rotation within the body axis is the result. This, together with the inability to raise the head and extend the spine, prevents turning over from supine to prone lying. Later on, it will interfere with the child's ability to sit up from the prone position. Up to the age of one year or even longer, a normal child when supine will sit up and stand up from supine by first turning over into prone lying, unless he is allowed to pull himself up to sitting with his hands. A child deprived of this ability to rotate within his body axis will, therefore, not be able to sit or stand up from supine unless his head and arm control are sufficiently normal to allow him to push or pull himself up to sitting.

Because of the insufficient elaboration of the early total patterns of both flexion and extension, the child will not be able to sit with erect spine and flexed hips, to kneel, or to crawl. He will not be able to stand up from prone-lying as he cannot raise his head or support himself on extended arms and hands.

Children in whom the condition is less severe and whose body is only partly affected, will develop at a slower rate than the normal child and will be held up at certain stages of development.

In time, the primary picture of abnormal co-ordination of posture and movement will undergo secondary changes. In the individual case, especially the milder one which has greater scope for compensation, these changes may be considerable. Certain individual variations are the result of the interplay among relevant tonic reflexes with their relative strengths. Individual variations are also due to the co-existence of normal primitive reactions and abnormal postural reflexes, and to the degree to which the latter interfere with the former. Moreover, changes in the primary picture will result from the child's efforts at compensation when he will adapt the abnormal patterns to functional use. The intelligent child will make use of his abnormal patterns; he will compensate for the shortcomings of more involved parts by excessive use of the less affected ones. The result is an obscuring of the primary picture and a greater complexity and individuality of the abnormal patterns. For instance, a child with fair head control will compensate for insufficient flexion of the hips in sitting with a dorsal kyphosis (Fig. 20 a), or for insufficient hip extension in standing with a lumbar lordosis (Fig. 20 b).

The Floppy Infant

Difficulties may be experienced in the early recognition of the hypotonic type of cerebral palsy, the so-called 'floppy infant'. In most cases of this type, hypotonia is a transitory symptom followed sooner or later by a fluctuating type of postural tone characteristic of the athetoid group, or by a spastic or plastic hypertonus. Hypotonia of central origin is usually seen in young babies who do not as yet try to move and are not yet responding to environmental stimulation. It is often present in mentally subnormal children, in whom it may remain unchanged for many years, or in pure cases of cerebellar ataxia, not strictly belonging to the cerebral palsies. There is little resistance or response to passive stretch of muscles and therefore an increased range of passive movement. Because of this, the child shows little discomfort if placed in what would normally be an uncomfortable posture. He has, therefore, little urge to move and to right himself. Increase of postural tone, even to hypertonus, though

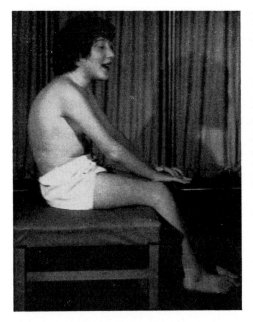

Fig. 20a. Spastic diplegia. In sitting, insufficient hip flexion with compensatory kyphosis.

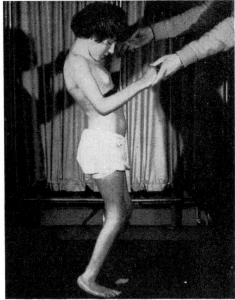

Fig. 20b. Spastic diplegia. In standing, insufficient extension and tilting forward of hips with compensatory lordosis.

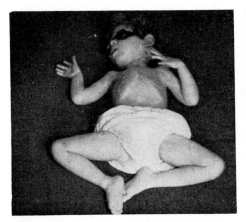

Fig. 21. A 'floppy' child. Note the retraction of the shoulders and the typical position of the legs.

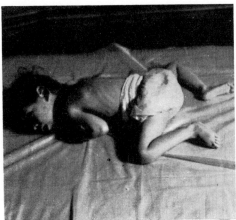

Fig. 22. The 'floppy' infant in prone-lying.

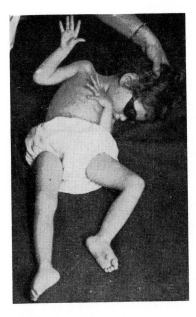

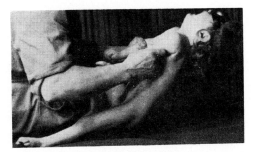

Fig. 24. (above). 'Dystonic' or 'opisthotonic' attack.

Fig. 23. (left). 'Floppy' child: retraction of the shoulders prevents turning to the side.

fleeting in nature, can nevertheless be produced by adequate stimulation.

During the first few months the baby usually lies on his back with widely abducted lower limbs flexed at the hips and knees, the thighs resting on the support. The feet are dorsiflexed and everted and can easily be dorsiflexed to touch the shin of the leg, a pattern which disappears in the normal baby after the first few weeks. The arms are abducted, outwardly rotated and flexed at the elbows (also a primitive baby pattern) (Fig. 21). When pulled up to sitting, the head lags far behind, much more so than in normal babies. When placed in prone he may not even turn his head to one side. The arms and legs are spread out sideways in extreme abduction and flexion, and the groin touches the support (Fig. 22). He is unable to turn from supine to side-lying, the neck righting reaction being absent (Fig. 23). He does not kick, and he moves his arms only feebly, if at all. Postural tone is insufficient to withstand gravity.

At later stages, as the child starts to react to stimulation, to being handled and moved about, postural tone develops, but not normally. He may then develop intermittent fluctuations of postural tone of varying amplitude. These will tend towards exaggerated extension in supine, when the child responds to handling by throwing himself backwards in a total extension pattern, called 'dystonic attacks' by Ingram (1955) and 'opisthotonic attacks' by Polani (1959) (Fig. 24). These attacks may also occur in supported sitting, when the child's head drops back. The child is unable to raise his head in either prone or supine.

The early recognition of this type of cerebral palsy and its differentiation from other causes of hypotonia rests on the interpretation of the child's response to handling. This aims at discovering early any potential hypertonic reactions to stimulation. Handling in supine and supported sitting may provoke excessive extensor activity — the influence of the tonic labyrinthine reflex — and also at times responses characteris-

19

Fig. 25. 'Floppy' child: legs in wide abduction, arms pull up in flexion.

tic of the asymmetrical tonic neck reflex. Flexor hyperactivity in prone may be demonstrated by raising the baby up by his shoulders. His arms will pull upwards in flexion against gravity (Fig. 25), indicating that the child's inability to raise his head may not only be due to the general hypotonic condition but to hyperactivity of the flexors. A valuable diagnostic sign has been described by Lesny (1960): namely, if the baby is held in vertical suspension with his feet above the ground, he may pull up his legs in flexion against gravity.

CHAPTER IV

Factors in the Assessment of Cerebral Palsy

While strongly agreeing with Milani-Comparetti (1964) that a study of the 'patterns' is of utmost importance, giving as it does valuable clues with respect to early diagnosis, classification, assessment, re-assessment and treatment, I feel that other factors cannot be altogether disregarded. They will give valuable additional information, especially with regard to the planning of a programme of treatment. Three factors, at least, should be considered in every case of cerebral palsy. Together they will determine the individual picture. These factors are:—

1. The type and strength of the abnormal muscle tone;
2. The type of disturbance of reciprocal innervation;
3. The distribution of the condition and the prevailing patterns of posture and movement.

It is perhaps not surprising that Milani-Comparetti places the emphasis on patterns of posture and movement, as his concepts are based on a study of young babies with cerebral palsy. In these patients abnormal qualities of postural tone are not yet very distinct, and the main problem of treatment is, therefore, one of 'reconstruction of patterns following the developmental sequence' rather than one of inhibition of abnormal patterns of posture and movement together with the facilitation of normal motor patterns. Treatment in the very young can forestall the development of the full picture of abnormality, and inhibition of abnormal patterns plays here a minor part.

1. Abnormal Muscle Tone

All cases of cerebral palsy have in common an abnormal muscle tone. This is classically examined by passively moving the segments of a limb and testing the resistance which the muscles offer to passive stretch. It is unfortunate that, so far, modern neurophysiology has not been able to explain the different types of abnormality of muscle tone seen in different types of cerebral palsy.

Sufficient is known about the nature of spasticity, which is considered to be the result of a release of the gamma-system, or more rarely the alpha-system, from higher inhibitory control (Rushworth 1960). Presumably the release of a facilitatory mechanism within the brain stem enhances the sensitivity or 'bias' of the gamma-system (Magoun and Rhines 1946). This becomes hyperexcitable and reacts to an adequate stretch in a maximal manner, that is, with a synchronised total discharge. The result is a synchronised excitatory phase followed by a synchronised phase of post-excitatory inhibition. After the passing of this phase one of post-inhibitory excitation returns. These observations may be the explanation of clinically observed phenomena of spastic muscle, that is the exaggerated stretch reflex, the clasp-knife phenomenon and the lengthening and shortening reactions.

21

More difficult is the explanation of rigidity. This term is unfortunate, as this type of hypertonus in cerebral palsy is different from the rigidity of Parkinson's disease. It is probably nearer the type of rigidity described by Sherrington and obtained by decerebration. This type of hypertonus is actually a severe degree of spasticity. In fact, all the laws of spasticity have been studied on decerebrate animals. Rigidity in cerebral palsy, perhaps better called 'plastic hypertonus', is characterised by the unchanging resistance a muscle offers to passive stretch throughout its whole range in the direction of either flexion or extension (The Little Club Memorandum 1959). This phenomenon may be caused partially by co-contraction (see point 2 below).

It is as yet impossible to explain the nature of the fluctuating type of muscle tone found in the athetoid group of cerebral palsy. The amplitude of fluctuation may vary widely in the individual case, either on the basis of a general hypotonic condition or of a fairly normal postural tone.

Flaccidity of muscle tone, hypotonia, is usually a transient phenomenon in cerebral palsy, occurring in earliest babyhood, and followed sooner or later by a spastic or plastic type of hypertonus or by the fluctuating tone of the athetoid group. The explanation of this type of muscle tone, resulting from a central lesion, may be a high threshold of the gamma-system to stimulation due to an over-active inhibitory centre in the brain-stem released from cerebellar control. These children may show considerable increments of muscle tone under sufficiently strong, long-lasting, or repetitive stimulation. This type of hypotonia is commonly found in cases of cerebellar ataxia — not strictly speaking belonging to the cerebral palsies. There is, however, an element of ataxia in some children of the athetoid group, especially those with a basically low postural tone.

The assessment of the type and strength of the myotatic response to stretch may be of some value in the diagnosis and classification of cases. It is, however, of very little value in assessing and re-assessing patients, or in the planning of treatment. For this one may mention the following reasons:—

1. Hypertonus and hypotonus as muscular phenomena are very variable, changing with the child's general condition and excitability and with the strength and speed of muscle stretch.

2. Different types of abnormality of muscle tone may be observed in the same child in different parts of the body.

3. One type of abnormal muscle tone in the same affected parts may change in time. This will necessitate re-assessment and reclassification of the case.

4. The strength and distribution of hypertonus in any particular part of the body change with alterations of the position of the head in space or of the relative position of head and neck in relation to the trunk, as a result of tonic reflex activity.

2. Disturbance of Reciprocal Innervation

A study of the law of reciprocal innervation and of the type of disturbance caused by an abnormal interplay of opposing muscular forces may be of great value in differentiating the various types of cerebral palsy, and offer valuable additional clues to treatment. It will also explain, at least to some extent, the reasons for the imbalance of opposing muscular forces which the orthopaedic surgeon finds so difficult to assess when dealing with the surgical problems of this condition (Blundell Jones 1961, Sharrard 1961). This problem is also discussed by Tardieu (1961).

Sherrington (1913) stressed the importance of reciprocal innervation for the regulation of postural tone in the maintenance of posture and the performance of normal movements. He showed that in spinal animals in the reflex co-ordination, for instance, of the flexor withdrawal reflex, the agonists were excited and contracted while simultaneously the antagonists were inhibited and relaxed. This phenomenon he called 'reciprocal inhibition'. He stated that inhibition was a central nervous phenomenon. He further stated that 'reciprocal inhibition' as studied on spinal animals was an artefact, a very special case of reciprocal innervation, not likely to occur under normal conditions.

In normal circumstances agonists, antagonists and synergists are pitted against each other in a much more adapted reciprocal interaction than that which occurs in simple reciprocal inhibition. This is due to the regulating influence of higher centres in brain stem, midbrain, cerebellum and cerebral cortex on the spinal reflex mechanism of muscular co-ordination. The antagonists are inhibited and relax in a graded and adapted manner, in step with the contracting agonists, and in so doing exert an important steadying and guiding influence on the movement in progress. Synergic muscle groups are made to contract to steady and fix neighbouring joints, in order to give precision to the movement and optimal mechanical conditions for the interplay of opposing muscular forces. For instance, in a contraction of the flexors of fingers and thumb, as when grasping an object, the extensors gradually relax and the synergists raise the wrist and stabilise it in an extended position. Sherrington also showed that in certain circumstances the agonists and antagonists were in a state of simultaneous contraction by reciprocal innervation. This is especially so in the service of postural fixation, as when standing on one leg. Palpation of the muscle of the thigh of the standing leg will show this to be the case. This simultaneous contraction of agonists and antagonists Riddoch and Buzzard (1921) called co-contraction.

In a child with a spastic or plastic hypertonus there seems to be, on the one hand, a deviation of reciprocal innervation towards an excess of co-contraction, in which spastic agonists are opposed by equally or more spastic antagonists. This is especially so around proximal joints. On the other hand, there may be also a deviation towards an excess of reciprocal inhibition. The severe tonic inhibition of certain muscles by their very spastic antagonists will cancel out any attempt at a movement. These muscles will, therefore, appear to be 'weak'.

Both types of deviation can be seen in the same spastic child in different parts of the body. For instance it may be found that all the muscles around the shoulder are in spastic contraction with severe depression of the shoulder and fixation of the scapula and that there is resistance of the arms to elevation, to extension backwards, to movements forward and to horizontal abduction. Another example is the simultaneous spastic contraction of the flexors and extensors of the hips with resistance of the hips to both full flexion and extension. Examples of tonic reciprocal inhibition are the 'weak' dorsiflexors of the ankles and toes which are opposed by the spastic muscles of the calf, or, in equinovarus of the ankles, 'weak' peronei in opposition to spastic tibialis anticus and posticus.

Co-contraction may not be evident until the child attempts to move, when the effort will make him stiffen his limbs owing to the simultaneous contraction of agonists and antagonists. For instance, an attempt to raise the arm will only succeed in a further depression of the shoulder: These facts seem to explain the immobility and fixation of the spastic child in a few typical abnormal postures and his difficulties in moving. Movements, if at all possible, are limited in range and direction and require excessive effort.

In the athetoid and ataxic group of patients the deviation of reciprocal innervation seems to be towards an excess of unmodified reciprocal inhibition. Any attempts at a movement will lead to an immediate and excessive relaxation of the antagonists. The lengthening group of muscles are unable to hold and guide the movement. Lack of co-contraction is also responsible for the poor supporting action of the synergists. This explains the well-known excessive mobility and the lack of fixation and postural control in this group of patients. Their movements are characterised by poor control, extreme range, and poor co-ordination. This seems to be the reason why Hammond (1871) gave the name 'athetosis' to this condition, meaning 'no fixed posture'.

These two factors — the abnormal muscle tone and the disturbed reciprocal innervation — important though they are, can be considered only in conjunction with an analysis of the prevailing total patterns.

3. Prevailing Patterns of Posture and Movement

The regulation of muscle tone throughout the body for the maintenance of posture and movement is the function of the proprioceptive system. Postural reactions play a dominant role in the regulation of the degree and distribution of muscle tone. Most of these reactions are elicited by stimulation of the sensory end organs in our muscles and joints, and by the otoliths and semicircular canals of the labyrinths. Exceptions are the optical righting reactions and the body righting reactions acting on the body and on the head, these latter resulting from tactile stimulation of the body. Muscle tone is dependent on an intact proprioceptive reflex arc. The propriocep-tive end organs lie in the muscle itself and are stimulated by movements of the body (Fulton 1951).

Modern neurophysiology has steadily moved towards the concept that posture and movement interact to such an extent that they cannot be separated. Postural changes are part and parcel of every movement; indeed, movements themselves are only to be regarded as changes of posture. The patterns of the postural reactions which give us head control, rotation, body righting and balance reactions form the background of our most selective willed movements and skills. Furthermore, the patterns of co-ordination of these postural reactions are essentially the same as those of our basic movements.

A normal postural reflex mechanism serves a twofold purpose:—

1. The maintenance of our equilibrium in all positions and during all activities

involving changes of the position of the body as a whole or of parts of the body in relation to each other.

2. The fixation of parts of the body in support of and for the guidance of moving parts.

These functions are brought about through modification of the spinal mechanisms for the regulation of postural tone* by higher facilitatory and inhibitory influences from brainstem, midbrain, cerebellum, frontal and parietal lobes, and by a harmonious integration of exteroceptive and proprioceptive stimuli. In this way, alpha and gamma activity are properly pitted against each other; the required degrees of reciprocal innervation for posture and movement are produced, and the whole of the musculature of the body is activated in well co-ordinated patterns for skilled activity.

It is clear that a lesion of the brain will throw this balanced mechanism out of gear. It will interfere with the harmonious interplay of higher facilitatory and inhibitory processes on the spinal reflex mehanism of control of postural tone. The type of disturbance will then depend on the degree and quality of this interference and on the extent to which facilitatory or inhibitory influences from above are withdrawn. In this way the brain lesion will produce the various types of abnormal postural tone, will interfere in varied ways with the interplay of alpha and gamma activity and will also lead to abnormal patterns of co-ordination.

It is important to appreciate that the same lesion which in experimental animals leads to a release of hypertonus also releases the patterns of the tonic reflexes. Decerebration sets free the centres of facilitation and inhibition of the brain stem (Magoun and Rhines 1946), which regulate postural tone by influencing the spinal reflex mechanism. This leads to over-activity of the various tonic or static reflexes — myotatic, segmental and general — with the resultant typical abnormal patterns of posture and movement in association with an abnormal postural tone.

It seems logical, therefore, to assume that hypertonus and the abnormal patterns of co-ordination are co-existent and are the expression of one and the same lesion. In other words, the various types of abnormal postural tone and their patterns of co-ordination are the expression of a 'short-circuiting' of all sensory input into the pattern of released and abnormal postural reflex activity.

This fact of the co-existence of abnormal postural tone and typical abnormal patterns of co-ordination has great practical significance. It forms the basic concept of a treatment which aims at obtaining more normal postural tone throughout the affected parts or the whole body by counteracting and stopping the abnormal patterns. Specific techniques of handling the child aim at preventing motor responses to sensory input from being channelled into the patterns of abnormal postural reflex activity.

Obviously one can look upon the problem of the abnormal muscle tone in cerebral lesions from different points of view. One can, for instance, regard it as a local muscular phenomenon and test the quality and degree of resistance of a muscle to passive stretch. Although scientifically correct, this way of evaluating muscle tone, normal and abnormal, will not give any reliable information as to function, nor does it form a

---

*The term 'postural tone' is used here to stress the function of muscle tone, that is, the maintenance of posture and equilibrium.

25

useful basis for a rational and adequate treatment. In physiotherapy, orthopaedics, and surgery, it has led to the emphasis being placed upon individual muscles and joints of a limb and on effecting local postural changes. This 'peripheral approach' disregards the fact that spasticity does not reside in one or two muscle groups of a limb, but is co-ordinated in patterns involving all the muscles of the affected parts of the whole body.

CHAPTER V

Tonic Reflexes

The tonic reflexes of particular relevance in cerebral palsy are the following:—

1. The tonic labyrinthine reflex
2. The tonic neck reflexes
    (a) the asymmetrical tonic neck reflex
    (b) the symmetrical tonic neck reflex
3. Associated reactions (Walshe 1923)
4. The positive and negative supporting reactions.

They have been described in great detail in previous publications (Bobath and Bobath 1959, 1962, 1964, 1965.)

1. The Tonic Labyrinthine Reflex

This reflex is evoked by changes in the position of the head in space, probably by stimulation of the otolith organs of the labyrinths. In the child with cerebral palsy it causes maximal extensor tone (thence hypertonus) in the supine position, and minimal extensor hypertonus with a relative increase of flexor tone in the prone position. Intermediate degrees of extensor hypertonus are produced by positions of the head between these two extremes, for instance, in sitting.

In the child with a severe spastic quadriplegia, extensor hypertonus in the supine position may be very strong. The head, neck and spine are retracted, the shoulders pulled back, the arms abducted and flexed at the elbows, and the lower limbs extended, inwardly rotated and adducted (Fig. 26 *a, b*).

This extensor hypertonus in the supine position prevents the child from raising his head and sitting up. Furthermore, the child cannot move his arms forward to grasp a support and pull himself up to a sitting position. He cannot bring his arms forwards and together in midline, and he cannot touch his body or bring his hands up to his mouth. If he turns his head to one side and tries to turn to this side, the retraction of his shoulders will prevent this.

When lying prone the child usually shows flexor hypertonus; his head and spine are flexed, his shoulders are pulled forwards and down, and his arms are caught under the body in flexion with his hands fisted (Fig. 27 *a, b*). The hips and knees are often flexed, but if the hips are extended the knees are usually extended as well. The child cannot raise his head and often cannot turn it to one side. He cannot extend his arms, and cannot extend his spine sufficiently to free his arm from under the body for support (Fig. 27*c*). Therefore, he cannot get himself up to the kneeling position.

It has been stressed before that, although extensor hypertonus is always strongest in the supine position and flexor hypertonus is most pronounced in the prone position, the effect of the tonic labyrinthine reflex depends on the child's initial type of hypertonus. In some children extensor hypertonus is so strong that it might be still present,

Fig. 26a. Primary posture of extensor spasticity in supine with severe spastic quadriplegia.

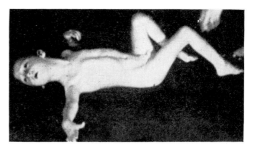

Fig. 26b. Secondary change of posture in hips and legs with severe co-contraction. Note also an asymmetrical tonic neck response on arms and legs.

Fig. 27a. Flexor spasticity in prone.

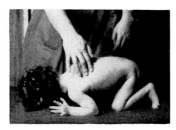

Fig. 27b. Flexor spasticity in prone.

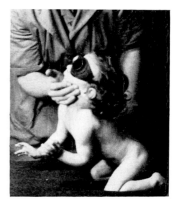

Fig. 27c. Flexor spasticity in prone: arms pull up in flexion, preventing protective extension of arms.

28

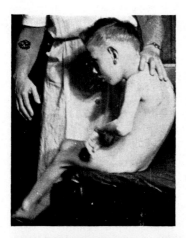

Fig. 28. Insufficient hip flexion in sitting compensated by kyphosis to bring the body over the sitting base. See also the asymmetrical tonic neck response in sitting.

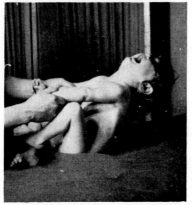

Fig. 29a. Spastic quadriplegia with some distal athetosis. Head raising in sitting increases extension; the child falls backwards.

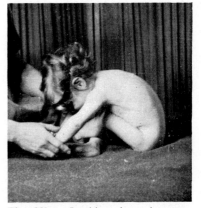

Fig. 29b. Looking down increases flexion; the child slumps forward into total flexion.

though to a greatly lessened degree, even in prone lying. Other children may show strong initial flexor hypertonus. They will show some degree of flexor hypertonus even when lying supine.

If the spastic child tries to sit, he may succeed by compromising between extensor and flexor hypertonus. Since he cannot flex his hips sufficiently, he will sit with semi-extended hips and bring his trunk forwards in a compensatory kyphosis (Fig. 28). If he has sufficient head control, his head may be held in a fairly normal position with the chin jutting out.

If the arms are not badly affected, the child will rely on them for support and will dislike taking both hands away from the support. He therefore uses only one hand unless he is well supported. If both arms are badly affected, they are drawn up in flexion. Raising the head and lifting the arms forwards and upwards will increase extensor hypertonus generally, and the child will fall backwards (Fig. 29 a); lowering the head will increase flexor hypertonus and the child will slump forwards (Fig. 29 b).

29

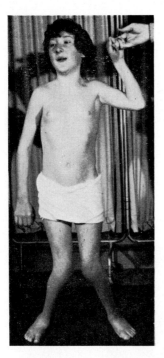

Fig. 30. Spastic diplegia.
Typical scissors posture.

Maintenance of the sitting posture is made still more difficult by the narrow sitting base produced by the adductor hypertonus of the legs and the lack of balance. In time the child may develop flexor contractures of his hips and knees and a permanent kyphosis.

Once the child has achieved the sitting posture in spite of the opposing forces of flexor and extensor hypertonus, the picture becomes one of a combination of both types of hypertonicity and the pattern of either total flexion or extension cannot be seen. In the same way the original picture of extensor hypertonus of the legs is changed in standing and walking to that of the well-known scissors posture (Fig. 30). To avoid falling backwards the child will flex his head and trunk forwards, thus introducing an element of flexion throughout the body, which particularly affects the hips and knees.

2 (a). The Asymmetrical Tonic Neck Reflex

This is a proprioceptive response obtained from the muscles of the neck and probably from the sense receptors of the ligaments and joints of the cervical spine as well. Turning the head to one side increases extensor hypertonus on the side to which the face is turned (the face limbs) and increases flexor hypertonus in the opposite limbs (the occiput limbs). In the severe case of cerebral palsy the response is an almost immediate one — the face limbs extend and the occiput limbs flex (Fig. 31 *a, b*). In milder cases there may be delay owing to a latency period, the length of which is inversely related to the severity of the case. The effect is usually more clearly seen in the arms than in the legs, and sometimes can be seen only in the arms (Fig. 31 c). It can often be more clearly demonstrated by an active movement of the child's head than by passive rotation. In some milder cases the reflex is present only when the child tries to do something difficult, or when he is excited. Sometimes it can be demonstrated only by testing the change of resistance of an arm to passive flexion or extension when the head is turned to one side and then away from it. In a diplegic child the effect of the asymmetrical tonic neck response may be observed only in the legs.

The asymmetrical tonic neck response may prevent the child from grasping an object while looking at it. In order to grasp the object, the child has to turn his head away from it. He also cannot bring his fingers to his mouth because he can bend his elbow only when his head is turned away from the arm. Often his eyes are fixed towards the side to which the face is turned, and he cannot look the opposite way or follow an object beyond the midline. The asymmetrical tonic neck response is usually stronger

30

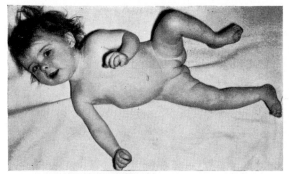

Fig. 31a.

Fig. 31b.

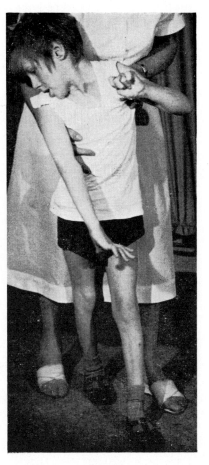

Fig. 31c.

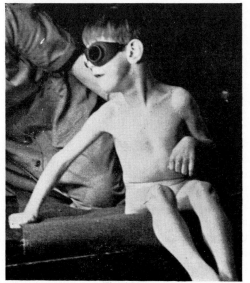

Fig. 31d.

Fig. 31a. Early abnormal asymmetrical tonic neck response on arms and legs. Note: asymmetry involves the trunk also. The legs are still in an attitude of abduction and outward rotation (primitive pattern).

Fig. 31b. Asymmetrical tonic neck response, involving arms and trunk, in a case of spastic quadriplegia with distal athetosis.

Fig. 31c. Asymmetrical tonic neck response in standing (supported), in a case of athetoid quadriplegia.

Fig. 31d. Asymmetrical tonic neck response in sitting and its volitional use for support. Athetoid quadriplegia.

31

on the right side. Most children with an asymmetrical tonic neck response therefore use their left hand. This is probably why many such children appear to be left-handed. An intelligent child, who learns to make use of the pattern of the asymmetrical tonic neck response for purposive activity in sitting (Fig. 31 *d*), will in time add a scoliosis to the kyphosis described above. There is also an additional danger of a subluxation of the hip joint of the occiput leg.

The influence of the asymmetrical tonic neck response can be seen in normal babies up to the age of four months or so. It is, however, very weak and shows itself only in the occasional assumption of the 'fencing position' from which the normal baby can easily move away, and which does not prevent him from sucking his fingers, whereas the child with cerebral palsy is stiff and more or less fixed in this position.

2 (b). The Symmetrical Tonic Neck Reflex

This is also a proprioceptive response evoked from the proprioceptors of the neck muscles by an active or passive movement of raising or flexing the head. Raising the head produces an increase of extensor hypertonus in the arms and of flexor hypertonus in the legs. Lowering the head has the opposite effect.

When the child with cerebral palsy is placed on his knees he usually shows a total picture of flexion and cannot extend his arms (Fig. 27*c*). However, if his head is passively raised he may extend his arms but his legs will be fixed in flexion, owing to the influence of the symmetrical tonic neck reflex (Figs. 32 *a*, *b*, *c*). Some children in whom the symmetrical tonic neck reflex is stronger than the tonic labyrinthine reflex cannot kneel with their head down, for their legs will then extend and their arms flex (Figs. 32 *d*, *e*).

The severely affected quadriplegic child usually shows so much flexor hypertonus when lying prone that he cannot get up to the kneeling position. In this case the tonic labyrinthine reflex dominates. The less affected quadriplegic and the diplegic children may get themselves into the kneeling posture by making use of the symmetrical tonic neck reflex pattern. They can, therefore, sit on their heels with the head raised and take their weight on extended arms, but they cannot extend their lower limbs at hips and knees to get to four-foot kneeling or move them alternately as in crawling. They may look fairly normal when sitting on their heels, but can only progress on the flexed lower limbs by pulling themselves forwards with the help of their arms.

3. Associated Reactions

Associated reactions, sometimes called associated movements, can be seen in normal people when they take strenuous exercise, for instance when lifting a heavy weight. They are tonic reactions acting from one limb on the other (Walshe 1923), and in the cerebral palsied child they produce a widespread increase of spasticity in all parts of the body not directly concerned with the movement. In the quadriplegic patient the effort of moving one limb will increase hypertonus in the rest of the body. If a hemiplegic patient squeezes an object with his sound hand, hypertonus will increase in the hemiplegic side and will show itself in an accentuation of the hemiplegic posture (Figs. 33 *a*, *b*). This means that in treatment one should not make the child

Fig. 32a.

Fig. 32b.

Figs. 32a, b. Symmetrical tonic neck response with raised head, arms in spastic extension and legs locked in flexion.

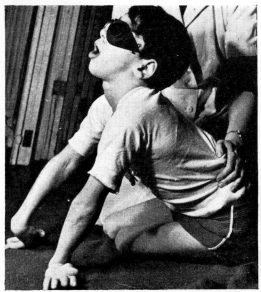

Fig. 32c. Symmetrical tonic neck response in athetoid quadriplegia.

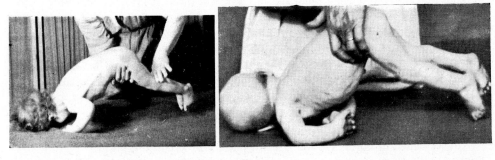

Fig. 32d. Symmetrical tonic neck response with head down, arms flexed and legs extended.

Fig. 32e. Symmetrical tonic neck response with head down, arms flexed and legs extended. The child is being lifted by the pelvis from prone-lying. Spastic quadriplegia.

33

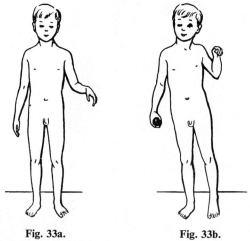

Fig. 33a.   **Fig. 33b.**

Figs. 33a, b. Associated reactions; left-sided hemiplegia, before and after squeezing a rubber ball with
healthy hand.

use any one part of his body with effort, because in trying to improve the function of
one part one may make the rest of the body worse. For instance, by trying to get
extension of the spastic arm of a hemiplegic child one may increase the extensor hypertonus of the spastic leg.

4. The Positive Supporting Reaction

The positive supporting reaction is the tonic modification of the spinal extensor
thrust, making a rigid pillar of a limb for weight-bearing (reflex standing). It is produced by a twofold stimulus:—

    1. Tactile, that is, by the touch of the ball of the foot on the ground.

    2. Proprioceptive, that is, by pressure resulting in a stretch of the intrinsic
       muscles of the foot.

As a result, muscle tone in the lower limbs increases in both the flexor and extensor groups of muscles (co-contraction) but more so in the anti-gravity muscles. The leg
stiffens and becomes a rigid pillar for support. The effect persists as long as the two
types of stimuli are active.

Under normal conditions the positive supporting reaction occurs in man only in
a very modified form. Standing on one leg will produce co-contraction of the muscles
of that limb. However, the limb still remains mobile in all joints, and the child is able
to flex hip, knees and ankle separately to any required degree without collapsing.

In attempting to stand, the spastic child touches the ground with his foot and
exerts pressure on the foot within the reflexogenic area of the positive supporting
reaction. He is prevented from putting his heel to the ground by an upsurge of extensor
spasticity which produces the well-known pattern of extension, inward rotation and
adduction of the whole of the standing leg with plantar flexion of the foot. The standing
base is, therefore, narrow and small. Pressure of the foot against the ground tends to

34

throw the child backwards and makes weight transfer over the standing leg difficult. If he raises one leg to make a step, extensor spasticity in the standing leg will increase still further. When he puts the raised leg down again to take the body weight, extensor spasticity in the standing leg will diminish and it may flex. Both these results are due to the added influence of the crossed extension reflex on the positive supporting reaction.

The athetoid patient usually lacks a sustained extensor tone and the co-contraction necessary for standing. The positive supporting reaction is absent, and the patient uses the pattern of the crossed extension reflex for walking. He can only stand on stiffly extended legs and in walking raises his legs too high in a total pattern of flexion.

The Interplay of Tonic Reflexes

A knowledge of the individual reactions is a great help in analysing the motor behaviour of children with cerebral palsy, and in recognising the influence of each postural reflex on the co-ordination of each child's postures and movements. Though these reflexes can rarely be seen in isolation, since the motor patterns observed are the result of a combination of responses acting simultaneously, certain distinct patterns of reaction which recur in the same circumstances can be traced to the dominating influence of one or the other single postural reflex.

It is comparatively easy to see this in the severely spastic patients who show released tonic reflexes most clearly. Such a patient can only learn to sit by himself if he has sufficient head control. This will enable him to strike a balance between flexor and extensor reflex activity. He can only learn to walk if his arms and trunk are less affected than his legs. He can then modify the extensor hypertonus of his lower limbs by thrusting his head and trunk forwards and by semi-flexing his hips and knees (Fig. 33). He will also use his head and trunk to compensate for the lack of balance reactions in his lower limbs and will use his hands excessively for support.

In athetoid children tonic responses of varying strength appear only momentarily and interfere with their voluntary movements.

In the less severe cases of athetosis and spasticity only traces of the typical tonic reflex patterns can be seen, because these children show more varied and adequate postural reactions and are capable of a great variety of voluntary movements. The abnormal responses proper usually cannot be elicited, but their combined influence can often be traced in the child's movement patterns. For instance, even a slightly spastic or athetoid child will walk with his legs inwardly rotated and will put his toes to the ground first.

CHAPTER VI

Interpretation of Clinical Findings

For the purpose of evaluating the type and degree of disability in the various types of cerebral palsy, one usually assesses the following:—
    1. the power of contraction of individual muscles, and
    2. the range of movement at any particular joint.

The Power of Contraction

When describing the motor deficit resulting from cerebral lesions the term 'weakness' is frequently used. Its meaning, however, is far from clear. The reasons for this 'weakness' may be varied, as is shown by the following:

(i) *Released Gamma System*

Weakness may be caused by hyper-sensitivity of the released gamma system, resisting alpha-activity. This is borne out by the fact that if gamma-overactivity can be stopped, for instance by the injection of a solution of phenol (Nathan 1959, Rushworth 1960), this inhibition can be removed, setting free a considerable potential for movement.

(ii) *Influence of Postural Pattern*

Muscles tested for power of contraction in one position may seem to be 'weak', but when tested in a different postural pattern may be made to contract. For instance, when the patient is asked to extend his elbow with his arm by the side of his body, his triceps seems to be weak. If, however, the arm is placed forward at the shoulder, he may well be able to extend his elbow, especially if his head is turned towards that side (as t.n.r.). Flexion of the arm at the elbow may now be 'weak' or impossible, as long as the arm remains flexed forward at the shoulder. If the forearm is now supinated passively flexion of the elbow may be possible, and extension will become weaker or impossible.

(iii) *Range of Contraction*

The strength and power of a muscle, as tested by an active movement, depends on the strength of opposing forces, and on the range within which the muscle is made to contract. Whereas normal or hypotonic muscle contracts best from a position in the outer range (of length), the 'weak' muscle contracts more easily in the inner range. The reason for the relative 'weakness' of spastic muscle in the outer range seems to be that it is then opposed by a spastic antagonist in the inner range.

For example, in the prone position flexion of the leg at the knee is possible once the angle between the thigh and leg is reduced to 90 degrees. In this position the knee flexors are in their inner range. However, when this angle is increased to greater than 90 degrees, the flexors of the knee are made 'weaker' by gravity as well as by extensor spasticity as the extensors increasingly begin to work in their inner range.

(iv) *Isolated Muscle Action*

A muscle may appear 'weak' only when made to work in isolation. An example of this is Phelps's (1941, 1954) 'confusion contraction' (synkinetic action). Active and passive flexion of the ankle is usually much easier as long as the leg is flexed in toto, the 'weak' tibialis anticus working quite well within the pattern of the total flexion reflex. In fact, even normal muscle works optimally only in certain patterns (Kabat 1952). Thus, in normal circumstances, closing of the fingers is associated with wrist extension which gives closure of the hand optimal power, while in the spastic and athetoid child grasp is difficult and 'weak' because there is usually an associated flexion and ulnar deviation of the wrist. In cerebral palsy, the ability of muscles to contract and work in only a reduced number of patterns prevents co-ordination in the wide range of normal functional patterns.

(v) *Sensory Deficit*

A contributory factor to 'weakness' of muscles in cerebral lesions may be sensory deficit or loss. This applies particularly to the spastic patient. The sensory side is not only responsible for initiating movements, but the guidance of the movement in progress is essentially the task of the proprioceptive system. The effect of sensory deficit on the performance of movements has been studied by Sherrington and Mott (1894/95) in monkeys by section of sensory roots to a limb. They found that 'from the time of performance of the section onwards, as long as the animal may be kept, the movements of the hand and foot are practically abolished'. It is also a well-known clinical experience that sensory loss can have a profound influence on the motor performance of a hemiplegic arm and hand. The techniques of increasing muscle power developed, for instance, by Kabat (1952) and Kabat and Knott (1948), rest largely on strong sensory stimulation.

The Range of Movement

When testing for the type and degree of hypertonus by assessing the range of a movement at any one joint, different results can be easily obtained by a change of the child's position. For instance, spastic resistance of the flexors of the wrist and fingers can be substantially diminished and the range of movement increased by elevating the upper limb of the child in supine lying, extending and outwardly rotating the upper arm and abducting the thumb. The degree of dorsi-flexion of the ankle can be increased more effectively and spasticity of the calf muscles reduced by testing the child in the standing position with the hips extended, the pelvis well forward, and with the knees extended and the weight of the body well over the forefoot, rather than by testing the extensibility of the calf muscles with the child on his back.

In the supine position, the resistance of the spastic hamstrings to flexion at the hips and extension at the knees may be very strong; the same strong resistance is felt if one tries to make the child sit up on the floor with extended knees (Fig. 34 *a*). However, if the resistance of the hamstrings is tested while the child is standing with his heels down, his legs abducted and his knees extended, he is often able to flex forward and touch the ground with his hands, especially if his weight is brought well for-

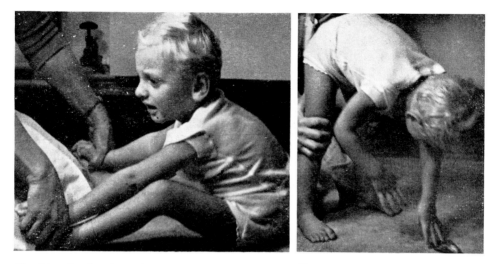

Fig. 34a. See description in text.   **Fig. 34b.** See description in text.

ward (Fig. 34 *b*). This seems to be due to the fact that as long as the child is tested in positions favouring extensor spasticity, as for instance in the supine or sitting position, co-contraction of the muscles of trunk and hips will be produced with strong resistance of the hamstring muscles. However, if the total extensor pattern is broken up, as in the example of standing with heels down, legs abducted and knees extended, the spasticity of the hamstring muscles and their resistance to flexion of the thighs at the hips and extension of the legs at the knees is greatly reduced.

It is clear, therefore, that in cerebral palsy the assessment of the power of single muscle groups and the range of motion at any one joint will be unreliable, as the result of such tests depends largely on the degree of hypertonus. This has been shown to be variable, and not always predictably so. The unreliability may be less in cases of long standing who have contractures and in whom structural changes in joints and changes in muscles have occurred. Furthermore, both muscle power and joint range have been shown to depend on the pattern within which any muscle is made to contract. A muscle may appear 'weak' when tested in isolation or as part of a pattern which is opposed by spastic antagonists. It may, however, contract easily and quite strongly in another pattern. The test response also depends on the position of the head in space and on changes of the position of the head. For these reasons, testing of muscle power and range of movement of individual muscle or muscle groups will not give much useful information as to how these muscles will perform in functional patterns. This is in agreement with Holt's statements (1965), that 'the functional activity cannot be predicted from the results of a clinical examination', and 'in many cases of cerebral palsy the response of muscles to stretch is unexpected, and unpredictable, and more complex than is often accepted'.

CHAPTER VII

Types of Cerebral Palsy

In the following, the various types of cerebral palsy, classified according to the three factors previously discussed, muscle tone, types of reciprocal innervation and postural patterns, will be considered. The motor development of each type will be sketched, and the influence of the abnormal postural patterns on the child's functional activities will be discussed with a description of the change of the primary patterns and the resulting contractures and deformities.

The Spastic Child

The spastic child shows hypertonus of a permanent character which may be either spastic or plastic. The degree of spasticity varies with the child's general condition, that is, his excitability and the strength of stimulation to which he is subjected at any moment. If spasticity is severe the child is more or less fixed in a few typical postures due to severe degrees of co-contraction of the involved parts, especially around the proximal joints. Some muscles may appear 'weak' as a result of tonic reciprocal inhibition, for instance, the glutei, quadriceps, dorsiflexors of the feet at the ankles, and the abdominal muscles. True weakness may, however, develop in some muscle groups because of disuse in cases of long standing. Spasticity is of a typical distribution and changes in a predictable manner, owing to tonic reflex activity. Movements are restricted in range and require excessive effort.

Spastic Diplegia or Paraplegia

In the diplegic child the lower extremities are more severely affected than the upper ones. The condition is usually of a fairly symmetrical distribution. Head control is usually good, and speech and articulation are not affected. If the arms are only slightly involved, these children are usually classified as 'paraplegias'. Not infrequently impairment of the co-ordination of the movements of the eyes can be observed.

During the first four or six months the baby may seem quite normal. Signs of spasticity may be absent or very slight. The physiological predominance of flexor tone and the baby's postural behaviour may be very similar to those of a normal baby of his age. He will develop normal righting of his head and, if the upper limbs are unaffected, normal protective reactions (propping reactions of the upper limbs). Any abnormality will show itself only when the normal process of development of extension reaches the lower trunk and hips. If the arms and head are slightly involved, the protective reaction of the upper limbs will appear late and will remain incompletely developed. Head raising in the prone and supine positions may then be difficult or delayed owing to flexor or extensor hypertonus respectively.

Though the arms may not show an asymmetrical tonic neck reflex, head turning may produce tonus changes in the legs. The child may kick only with the 'occipital' lower limb while the lower limb to which the face is turned may be held in extension—

first in a pattern of outward rotation, but later on the total spastic pattern of extension, adduction and inward rotation may develop. In the more severe cases this pattern of extension, adduction and inward rotation may develop very early, i.e. before the age of six months.

If the head and upper limbs are only slightly involved or even unaffected, the child may, during the early phase of predominant flexion, still be able to turn to his side. Rolling over to prone will, however, present difficulties. The child will learn this much later and will be able to do it only with the help of his arms while the lower limbs remain stiffly extended. The difficulty is largely due to a lack of rotation within the body axis and the inability to flex and bring the uppermost leg across. Once he has succeeded in rolling over to prone, he may learn to progress on his abdomen by a kind of swimming movement, i.e. by alternating abduction-flexion and adduction-extension movements of the lower limbs. At this stage the early normal primitive movements of the lower limbs may still persist in the prone position while in the supine and sitting positions the lower limbs may be in stiff extension.

Later on, creeping will become impossible as extension increases and as, at the same time, extensor spasticity of the lower limbs grows stronger. This happens at about the same time that the normal baby learns to extend his spine and hips sufficiently to support himself in prone on his forearms. The diplegic child will now progress by dragging himself along the floor with flexed arms and stiffly extended legs. The effort of pulling the body along in this way will increase extensor spasticity of the legs (associated reactions), and they will soon show the total extensor spastic patterns with extension, adduction and inward rotation.

Though the child may be able to raise his head in the supine position and to bring forward his arms and hands for grasping, sitting up will be difficult or impossible as his hips will resist flexion and his legs will adduct and may even cross. Sitting up alone may, therefore, be delayed up to the age of three years or longer. He may, however, be able to sit with support nearer the normal stage. In such a case early diagnosis may not be made until the baby is about eight or nine months old, that is, at a time when he should be sitting up by himself but does not do so properly and has poor sitting balance. Sitting fairly stably is only made possible by compensating for the insufficient flexion at hip and knee joints, i.e. by bringing the head and spine well forward. If the arms can be extended they will be used for support, since the child lacks equilibrium of the pelvis and lower limbs. The child will, at best, be able to use one arm and hand only for grasp, reach and play, and he will be unwilling to raise his head or reach out with both upper limbs as he will then tend to fall backwards.

In some cases a persistent Moro response may add to the difficulties by making it impossible for the child to put his hands down for support in stopping himself from falling backwards. In those children who are unable to use their upper limbs for support, the strong flexion of the spine will, in time, result in a structural kyphosis with flexor hypertonus of the neck, chest and abdominal muscles. The pelvis will be tilted forwards. The extensor spasticity at hips and knees with a relative reciprocal inhibition of the flexors will gradually be changed into a picture of co-contraction of flexors and extensors around the hip- and knee- joints. This is the beginning of the development of the well-known scissor posture of the lower limbs, later seen in standing. It will become more distinct in standing through the effect of the positive supporting reaction, which will add sufficient extensor tone for the child to stand.

The sitting pattern of the diplegic child whose upper limbs are relatively free will be different, as he can use them for support. He will use a pattern of strong flexion of the hips which helps him to abduct his thighs and flex his knees. The pelvis is tilted backwards and he sits with a stiffly extended spine. Later on, when standing up, extension at the hips will become difficult, and the child will then use extension of head and shoulders to assume and maintain the erect posture in spite of hip flexion. This results in a compensatory lordosis. He tends to fall backwards unless he can hold on to a support. As in the other type of diplegia, co-contraction of the muscles around the hips and knees will develop in standing and walking, with the resultant scissoring of the legs.

Whereas the normal child achieves a fair degree of emancipation of arms and hands around the eighteenth month, having by then acquired sufficient balance of trunk and legs, the diplegic child has to rely on his arms for support indefinitely. In early life he pulls himself along the floor, being either prone or kneeling; later, when learning to stand and walk, he has to hold on to people or furniture or has to use sticks or crutches. This involves constant and excessive use of the flexor muscles of arms and hands and also of the shoulder girdle and trunk, which are usually involved to some extent. He will, therefore, retain a clumsy grasp with pronation of the forearm; this is the primitive pattern of grasp and release belonging to the earliest stages of normal child evelopment when flexor patterns are still dominant. Extension of the hands at wrists and fingers, abduction and opposition of the thumb and supination movements of the forearm and hand will develop late and incompletely.

In standing and walking, which are acquired late and are only possible if arms and hands can be used, the diplegic children will make excessive use of whatever righting and equilibrium reactions are present 'above the waist'. They, therefore, use excessive compensatory movements of head, upper trunk and arms, as the legs and hips are stiff and comparatively immobile. They cannot shift their body weight automatically on to the standing leg to leave the other leg free to make a step. The body weight remains on the inside of the foot. They lack balance and rotation and seem to be falling from one leg to the other in walking; they are unable to stand still without holding on to something.

There seem to be two principal walking patterns:—

1. Children with strong flexion of the dorsal spine and a forward tilt of the pelvis lean backwards with their trunk in order to raise one leg and bring it forward to take a step. They then throw their body forward to transfer their weight (pigeon walk).

2. Children who show a straight and erect dorsal spine with a lordosis of lumbar spine (due to flexor spasticity around the hips, especially of the ilio-psoas) will use alternating side flexion of the trunk from the waist in order to bring the stiff legs forward. Whereas a normal person walks with mobile legs and a relatively stable trunk, these children show excessive mobility of the trunk and stiff legs.

Most diplegic children stand and walk on tip-toe, as dorsiflexion of the feet at the ankles would produce an increase of flexor tone throughout the lower limbs, which would make standing and walking impossible and might cause them to collapse.

Thus, as has been mentioned before, the lower limbs of an older diplegic child will show a pattern of mixed flexor and extensor spasticity, that is, co-contraction. The original pure pattern of extensor spasticity with a relative inhibition of all flexor activity has become modified in order to make standing and walking possible. With the original total extensor pattern the child could neither stand nor walk. He would fall backwards and would not be able to flex and lift one lower limb to transfer his body weight forward.

The deformities which may result from the functional use of the abnormal patterns are the following:—

1. A kyphosis of the dorsal spine.

2. A lordosis of the lumbar spine (Fig. 35).

3. Subluxation or dislocation of one or both hips due to adduction of the thighs and insufficient development of the hip joints — resulting from late standing.

4. Adduction and inward rotation of the legs with flexor deformities of hips and knees resulting in the typical scissors posture.

5. An equino-varus or -valgus deformity of the feet.

Fig. 35. Spastic diplegia with insufficient hip extension in standing and a compensatory lumbar lordosis. There is a dorsal kyphosis in order to bring the upper trunk and head over the standing base.

Spastic Quadriplegia

In this type of cerebral palsy the whole body is affected; the distribution is very asymmetrical, one side being more involved than the other and the upper limbs being more affected than the lower. For these reasons these cases have also been referred to as 'double hemiplegias'. The upper parts being more affected, head control is usually poor, and speech and articulation are more or less severely involved. If spasticity is severe the child is helpless and immobile. Any effort to move will produce 'associated reactions' and will therefore result only in further increases of spasticity, accentuating the abnormal posture.

Early recognition of these cases is not usually difficult. Both the retardation of normal motor development and abnormal signs of tonic reflex activity can be seen early. This is due to the fact that the neck and upper limbs are involved and, therefore, abnormal reflex activity interferes with the earliest signs of motor maturation, such as head control and the development of extension against gravity. Early diagnosis is made easier when the child presents with signs such as neck retraction in the supine position (soon followed by retraction of shoulders and stiff extension of the spine), a persistent and strong asymmetrical tonic neck reflex and an inability to raise (or often even to turn to one side) the head in the prone position. In milder cases this picture will develop more slowly and signs of abnormality may show themselves first in the more involved side only. An initial diagnosis of hemiplegia may, therefore, be made at this stage.

Once spasticity is fully developed, the child is unable to right his head, maintain his equilibrium in any position or to use his arms and hands. In supine lying he usually shows strong neck and shoulder retraction. Neck righting is absent and rotation of the head to one side may only lead to the assumption of an asymmetrical tonic neck reflex attitude. Any attempt of the trunk to follow the head and so to roll over to that side is prevented by the retraction of the shoulder. The child is, therefore, unable to roll from supine into side-lying. He lacks rotation within the body axis—the result of absence of the body righting reaction acting on the body — and cannot therefore roll over into prone lying. In prone lying, he is usually unable to raise his head, or to use his arms and hands for support, and therefore cannot get up. The shoulders and spine are flexed and the arms pull up in flexion if the body is lifted off the support by the shoulders. Thighs and legs may be flexed. However, if the thighs are extended at the hips, the legs will be extended, inwardly rotated and adducted. The feet will then be plantar flexed at the ankles.

Inability to raise the head prevents him from initiating sitting up. He cannot bring his arms forward and into midline to pull himself up to sitting. The difficulty in sitting up is further enhanced by the inability or difficulty in flexing his thighs at his hips, which results from a increase of extensor spasticity caused by the touch and pressure of the buttocks against the support.

Only a few of these children develop some righting ability of the head. This ability is interfered with by tonic reflex activity whenever the head is moved into a position which favours its occurrence. For instance, in trying to look up while sitting, the child raises his head high and will then fall backwards into extension, not infrequently throwing his arms up and out in a Moro response.

If head control is fair, the intelligent child may learn to avoid these danger positions. He may even learn to use his head for the neutralisation of tonic reflexes. For instance, if extensor and flexor spasticity are strong in the supine and prone positions respectively, he may learn to sit by moving his head into a mid-position, which allows sitting by creating a certain equilibrium between the two forms of spasticity. He will then lean slightly backwards, compensating for insufficient flexion of his hips by a kyphosis of the dorsal spine in order to bring trunk and head over the sitting base (Fig. 36 *a*, *b*). The neck will be hyperextended and the head held stiffly in a more or less normal position. The sitting base is narrow and precarious owing to the adduction-flexion attitude of the legs. He cannot use his arms for support, because he is unable to extend them. When attempting to raise his head, he is in danger of falling backwards; when looking down, he will slump forward.

43

If, in addition, the child has a strong asymmetrical tonic neck response, usually stronger to the right, he may learn to use one arm for grasp and release by turning his head first to one side to reach out and then to the other to grasp the object. Other children may adopt an attitude of full flexion in sitting. The head is flexed forward and they will look down in order to avoid the asymmetrical tonic neck reflex which is strongest in extension. They will in this way also avoid sudden startle reactions which upset their balance whenever they try to look up. They will now make use of the symmetrical tonic neck reflex which will enable them to use both hands for holding and grasping. They cannot, however, now extend their arms to reach out and the lower limbs will tend to extend and adduct. In order to sit, these children will therefore use excessive flexion of the spine and will in time develop a kyphosis of the dorsal spine and semi-flexion deformities of hips and knees with strong co-contraction of the flexors and extensors of hips and knees.

The quadriplegic child with moderate spasticity may in time acquire some of the righting and equilibrium reactions in sitting and kneeling but not in standing or walking. Unless the child can compensate for this lack of equilibrium by using his arms and

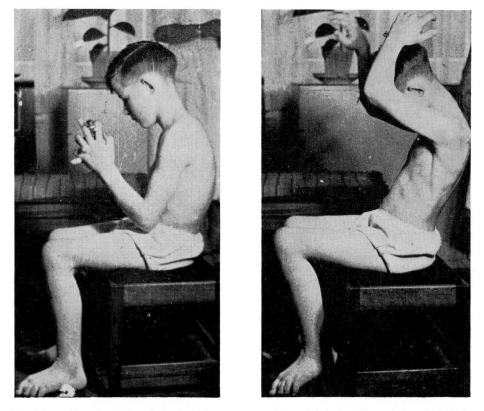

Fig. 36 *a* and *b*. A child with moderately severe spastic quadriplegia. When sitting there is insufficient hip flexion, compensatory kyphosis and slight flexion of the head. Raising the arms increases hip extension and increases the kyphosis and head flexion.

hands for support, standing and walking will be impossible. As long as the child in sitting moves slowly and carefully and avoids extreme positions, tonic reflex activity will not interfere greatly and postural tone may remain fairly normal.

The deformities likely to result from the child's use of tonic reflex patterns for functional activities may therefore be the following:—

1. A scoliosis or kypho-scoliosis,
2. Flexor deformities of hips and knees; an equino-varus or -valgus of the ankles,
3. Subluxation of one hip (rarely of both) usually the left hip. This may be the result of the following factors:
    a. Underdevelopment of the hip joints in a child who has never stood or walked,
    b. Adductor spasticity with a coxa vara and inward rotation of the legs,
    c. The pelvic tilt due to the asymmetrical distribution of the condition. On the side with more flexion, spasticity of the side flexors of the trunk will pull the pelvis up and rotate it forward. This tendency is accentuated by a strong asymmetrical tonic neck reflex. This is probably the most important factor.

The factors responsible for a subluxation or dislocation of the hips in cerebral palsy seem very complex. It seems that the imbalance of muscle power between the adductors and glutei, especially the gracilis and gluteus medius, is not the whole of the problem, and that the one-sided position of the child's head and the resulting asymmetry of trunk and pelvis play a major part.

Spastic Hemiplegia

The early diagnosis of spastic hemiplegia is usually not difficult because of the early asymmetry of postural and movement patterns. The affected hand is fisted and the baby does not open it. He does not kick with the affected leg. The head is usually turned away from the involved side. He does not pass through the symmetrical stage of normal baby development, beginning around the sixteenth week when the last vestiges of an asymmetrical tonic neck response influence disappear. He therefore does not use both hands in midline, does not reach out and grasp with the affected hand and does not support himself on the hemiplegic lower limb.

His development will be delayed in all activities which require balance of the trunk and use of both hands for support. It will take him longer than normal children to establish balance in sitting, standing and walking. He will show a tendency to fall towards the affected side, as he lacks balance reactions of limbs and trunk on that side; and he will be unable to protect his face when falling, as flexor spasticity prevents him from extending his affected upper limb (absence of protective extension reaction).

The child will gradually orientate himself towards the sound side; he will prefer in an emergency to fall towards that side because he is then able to protect his face and head. In due course righting and equilibrium reactions will even become hyperactive on the sound side, in order to compensate for their absence on the affected side.

At first the hemiplegic baby progresses along the floor in prone-lying, turning his head away from the affected side and dragging along the hemiplegic arm and leg. The affected limbs are either little used or cannot be moved at all. He does not learn to crawl on hands and knees but will learn to progress on his seat, pulling himself along with the sound arm and dragging the affected side along. He will only learn to sit up and stand up with the help of the sound side, and the establishment of equilibrium in standing and walking will be somewhat delayed.

In standing he will support his weight mainly on the sound leg. At first the affected leg will remain abducted and relatively free of weight. It will appear to be weak rather than spastic, and the child will tend to collapse on it because leg and foot are still mobile and he has therefore insufficient extensor tone to support his weight, as long as his heel is on the ground and his knee is flexed and mobile. This difficulty can best be observed when the child attempts to walk downstairs. He cannot do this in the normal way, that is, by stepping down with alternating use of his legs, but uses only the affected side for stepping down, while bearing his weight on the flexed sound leg. At this stage he can usually put his heel on the ground quite easily. Because of the abduction pattern of the whole lower limb at this stage, his foot shows eversion rather than inversion, though his toes are already stiff in plantar flexion and will 'claw.'

As the child learns to walk, the leg and foot will gradually stiffen as he will have to take his weight, at least momentarily, on the affected limb. He can only support his weight on the affected leg with the help of extensor spasticity, which is produced by the pressure of the ball of the foot against the ground. This means, however, that he has to walk on his toes. Extensor spasticity now gradually increases, and in many cases a pattern of inversion and plantar flexion of the ankle develops in addition to the 'clawing' of the toes.

In walking, the child is unable to dorsiflex his foot at the ankle sufficiently and as a result he will hyperextend his knee as he brings his weight forward over his foot. To allow him to put his heel to the ground, his pelvis is kept rotated backwards on the affected side and his hip fixed in some degree of flexion. He develops a pattern of walking very similar to his pattern of moving along the floor in the sitting position, dragging the affected side behind. At the same time flexor spasticity of the upper limb increases, largely as the result of associated reactions; the forearm pulls up in walking and even more so in running. Associated reactions result from efforts of the sound side, e.g. the exclusive use of the sound hand and over-activity of the sound leg, also from lack of balance and difficulty of raising the affected leg in walking. The opening of the fingers of the affected hand, for example, becomes increasingly difficult and possible only with a flexed wrist.

A hemiplegic child may in time develop the following contractures and deformities:—

1. Flexor deformities of elbow and wrist with pronation of the forearm and ulnar deviation of the wrist.
2. Adduction of the thumb.
3. Scoliosis of the spine. This is due to the spastic contraction of the side-flexors of the trunk on the affected side. It will produce a pelvic tilt, as the pelvis will be drawn up on the affected side (Fig. 37 *a, b*). The shoulder will be pulled down. This may be aggravated by shortening of the affected leg, owing to disturbances of growth through disuse or trophic impairment.
4. An equino-varus or -valgus of the ankle with shortening of the Achilles tendon.

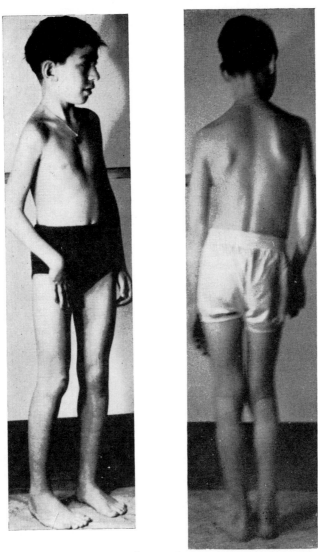

Fig. 37 *a* and *b*. Right hemiplegic child (photographed on two separate occasions) showing the typical deformities described in text.

The Athetoid Child

Common Features

All athetoid patients show an unsteady and fluctuating type of muscle tone, but the amplitude of the fluctuations may vary widely in the individual case. These children lack sustained postural tone and cannot, therefore, maintain a stable position. There is insufficient postural fixation due to a lack of co-contraction, that is, simultaneous contraction of agonists and antagonists, to give guidance and proper support to

47

the moving part. The grading of antagonistic activity during a movement is poor, and contraction of one group of muscles will lead to a complete relaxation by reciprocal inhibition of its antagonists. The lengthening groups do not hold and, therefore, do not grade the intended movement. Because of this the movements are jerky and extreme in range with poor control of the middle ranges.

Because of the lack of co-contraction and the extreme ranges of movement on the basis of a low postural tone, there is hyper-mobility of all joints with a tendency to subluxation, especially of the mandibles, the shoulder and hip joints, and the fingers.

Fluctuations of muscle tone are sudden and manifest themselves in some of the involuntary movements seen in all cases of the athetoid group. In the individual case we may see the following types of involuntary movements:

a. *Intermittent tonic spasms:* These are predictable in pattern, and are largely dependent on a change of the position of the head; that is, they are due to the influence of the tonic labyrinthine and neck reflexes. They may fix the child temporarily in certain extreme postures of total flexion or extension (tonic labyrinthine influence), or in assymmetrical postures of extension of the face limbs and flexion of the skull limbs (asymmetrical tonic neck reflex influence). There may be a mixture of both in the individual case.

b. *Mobile spasms* (Kinnier Wilson and Walshe 1914/15): These involve the limbs in alternating movements of flexion and extension, pronation and supination etc. They are often rhythmic in nature. Examples are the 'athetoid dance' (spinal stepping reflexes) and the pawing of the ground with one foot.

c. *Fleeting localised contractions:* They affect muscles or muscle groups anywhere in the body and if they are strong and affect many muscle groups, they may produce grotesque and exaggerated postures and movements, like the grimacing of the face, and the bizarre attitudes and movements of hands and fingers. Their patterns of co-ordination are quite unpredictable and the law of reciprocal innervation is in abeyance in this type of involuntary movement (Kinnier Wilson 1925). These postures and movements defy attempts at imitation by a normal person. If these localised muscular contractions are weaker and more limited they may show themselves only in minor localised twitches.

All these types of involuntary movement are reinforced during any attempt at volitional activity, when the patient tries to co-ordinate a purposeful movement against the background of an unstable postural tone and in spite of the interference by tonic reflexes.

Most of the cases of the athetoid group belong to the quadriplegias, in whom the head and upper parts are more involved than the lower ones. The distribution is usually asymmetrical, one side more involved than the other. A few cases are seen among the hemiplegias who show some distal athetosis; this appears usually around or after the sixth to seventh year. More rarely one sees children with a pure hemiathetosis.

In the athetoid quadriplegias postural tone is usually low during the first two to three years. Their postural patterns resemble those of a premature child rather than

48

those of a full term baby. Righting reactions may not develop for many years and may remain defective even in later life. Head control is absent or very poor, the baby being unable to raise his head in supine or prone lying. In the supine position he is unable to initiate sitting up or to turn over to prone or side lying. The baby cannot tolerate prone lying as he is unable to raise his head, extend his spine and hips or use his arms for support. He cannot get up on hands and knees and is unable to crawl. He may, therefore, spend the first years of his life in supine lying or propped-up sitting. He commonly holds his head to one side, usually the right, and cannot move it into midline or maintain it there. When pulled to sitting the child's head lags excessively. He is unable to lift it off the support and indeed pulls it backwards.

As the child grows older and starts to react more to environmental stimulation, postural tone develops and becomes stronger. He will now suddenly stiffen with increasing frequency and in the supine and sitting positions throw his head backwards with extension of hips and spine (Ingram 1955, Polani 1959). The patterns of these intermittent extensor spasms are often the only motor patterns in the supine position of which the child makes voluntary use for moving himself backwards along the floor. This he does by bending his legs and pushing his feet, which are less affected, against the floor. At this stage the asymmetrical tonic neck response activity is usually very strong and affects not only the upper limbs but the whole of the trunk. The resulting asymmetrical postural pattern produces a scoliosis with tilting of the pelvis, which is sometimes followed by a subluxation or dislocation of one hip (usually the left).

He usually retains a primitive flexion-abduction pattern of the lower limbs unless there is additional spasticity, in which case the legs will show a typical extension-adduction pattern. The retention of the abduction-flexion pattern makes sitting on the floor possible later on, as it gives the child a wide sitting base. Sitting is also made possible through some equilibrium reactions of the less affected hips and legs. Though he may not be able to pull himself to sitting, as he cannot lift his head or use his arms, when pulled to sitting he may assist in the movement by strong active flexion of the hips.

Though unable to control his head when being pulled to sitting, once he has reached the sitting position the child may be able to hold his head up and his spine erect, but his head will be turned to one side. In sitting he may learn to use one hand, usually the left, turning his head to the right and using the pattern of the asymmetrical tonic neck reflex for grasping. His grasp is usually weak, however, and he releases objects too easily and cannot hold on to a support. This is quite different from the tonic grasp of the spastic child, who cannot open his hands but holds on tightly to an object placed into his palm and, in fact, cannot release it.

Though the athetoid may be able to sit on the floor with extended and abducted legs, he cannot sit unsupported on a chair as this requires additional flexion of the knees. This would produce a total flexion pattern of the body resulting in the patient's falling forwards and down, especially if he could not use his arms and hands for support. If he raises his head in sitting, a total extensor pattern results and he falls backwards.

If the lower limbs are not too badly affected the child will learn to roll to his side and over to prone lying, initiating the movement with his legs. From the prone position, though he is unable to raise his head or to support himself on his arms, he will manage to get himself to a kneeling position by first pulling his legs in total flexion under his body. He can then raise his head and use his arms for support in extension, making use of the symmetrical tonic neck reflex. He can thus move into kneel-sitting, but he cannot alternately extend and flex his legs and is only able to hop along the floor in this position. Kneeling on all fours and normal crawling will be impossible.

Standing and walking will depend on the relative normality of the child's legs and on the degree of head control and equilibrium which he can develop. He usually cannot use his hands to hold on to a support, to pull himself up to standing or to hold on when walking. Extensor spasms tend to make him fall backwards, and both this and the asymmetrical distribution of postural tone interfere with balance. The constant fluctuations of postural tone make for insufficient support tonus. It may take him years to stand for any length of time and many children whose lower limbs are badly involved may not stand or walk at all. When they are made to stand, the legs are in a total extension-adduction pattern and may even cross. These children stand high on their toes, their neck and shoulders are retracted, and they tend to fall backwards. If they flex one leg to make a step, they may collapse in full flexion.

Other children whose lower limbs remain mobile and retain abduction, not only in sitting but also in standing, will learn to stand and even to walk. However, they use a primitive pattern of high stepping, lifting their legs too high. The abduction pattern of the lower limbs together with dorsiflexion and eversion of the feet will give them a sufficient walking base. They walk with hyperextended hips and knees and lean the trunk and shoulder girdle backwards to avoid collapse in flexion, in this way reinforcing extensor tonus (Fig. 38).

Many athetoids seem to have some element of ataxia. This applies especially to the athetoid with a basically low postural tone. The ataxic element, however, is difficult to differentiate from athetosis if involuntary movements are very marked. If athetosis is slight and distal in distribution, the ataxic element may be very clear. Athetosis, with its lack of a sustained postural tone, insufficiency of co-contraction and lack of a proper grading of 'reciprocal innervation', demonstrates a type of postural tone that is very similar to that seen in ataxia.

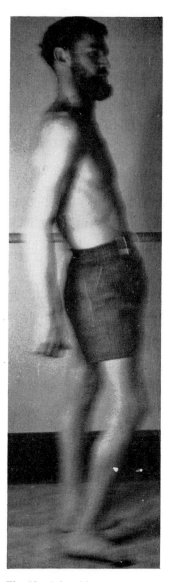

Fig. 38. Athetoid quadriplegia—typical walking pattern.

The athetoid child is not likely to develop deformities, as postural tone is generally low and he is mobile and has, in fact, too many patterns. However, because of his hypermobility he may show a tendency towards subluxation or dislocation of the mandible, shoulder and hip joints, and of the fingers.

The mixed cases of this group, that is, the athetoid with spasticity or the dystonic child with strong intermittent increases of postural tone, may, however, develop the following contractures or deformities:—

1. A scoliosis or kypho-scoliosis, often associated with deformities of the chest wall.
2. Flexor deformities of elbows and wrists, the wrists showing severe flexion with extended and 'weak' fingers.
3. Flexor deformities of hips and knees with equino-varus or -valgus of the ankles.
4. Dislocation of one or both hips, usually the left.

References

André-Thomas, Chesni, Y., Saint-Anne Dargassies, S. (1960) The Neurological Examination of the Infant. Little Club Clinics in Develop. Med. No. 1. London: Spastics Soc. pp. 21, 23, 31, 39, 41, 43, 45, 47.
——, Saint-Anne Dargassies, S. (1952) Etudes Neurologiques sur le Nouveau-Né et le jeune Nourrisson. Paris: Masson.
——, (1940) Equilibre et Equilibration. Paris: Masson.
Bazett, W. C., Penfield, W. G. (1922) 'A study of the Sherrington decerebrate animal in the chronic as well as acute condition.' Brain, 45, 185-265.
Blundell Jones, G. (1961) 'Dislocation of the hip in asymmetrical spasticity of the thigh adductors. Cerebral Palsy Bull., 3, 190.
Bobath, B. (1965) Abnormal Postural Reflex Activity caused by Brain Lesions. London: Heinemann.
Bobath, K. (1959) 'The neuropathology of cerebral palsy and its importance in treatment and diagnosis.' Cerebral Palsy Bull., 1, 13.
——, Bobath, B. (1964) 'The facilitation of normal postural reactions and movements in the treatment of cerebral palsy.' Physiotherapy, 50, 246.
——, —— (1964) 'Grundgedanken zur Behandlung der Zerebralen Kinderlahmung.' Beitr. Orthop. Traum., ii, (3), 1.
——, —— (1962) 'An analysis of the development of the standing and walking patterns in patients with cerebral palsy'. Physiotherapy, 48, 144.
——, —— (1956) 'The diagnosis of cerebral palsy in infancy.' Arch. Dis. Childh., 31, 408.
Clemessen, S. (1951) 'Some studies on muscle tone.' Proc. roy. Soc. 44, 642.
Fulton, J. F. (1951) Physiology of the Nervous System. New York: Oxford Univ. Press. pp. 115-132, 162-193.
Gesell, A., Amatruda, C. S. (1947) Developmental Diagnosis. 2nd ed. London: Harper.
Hammond, W. A. (1871) A Treatise on Disease of the Nervous System. New York: Appleton.
Holt, K. S. (1965) 'Facts and fallacies about neuromuscular function in cerebral palsy as revealed by electromyography.' Develop. Med. Child Neurol., 8, 255.
Illingworth, R. S. (1960) The Development of the Infant and Young Child, Normal and Abnormal. London: E. & S. Livingstone. p. 125.
Ingram, T. T. S. (1962) In R. W. B. Ellis, Child Health and Development. London: Churchill. pp. 183/4,
—— (1955) 'A study of cerebral palsy in the childhood population of Edinburgh.' Arch. Dis. Childh.. 30, 85.
—— (1955) 'The early manifestations and course of diplegia in childhood.' ibid, p.244.
Kabat, H. (1952) 'Studies in neuro-muscular dysfunction. XV. The role of central facilitation in restoration of motor function in paralysis.' Arch. Phys. Med., 33, 532.
——, Knott, M. (1948) 'Principles of neuromuscular re-education.' Phys. Ther. Rev., 28, 107.
Karlsson, B., Vassella, F. (1962) 'Asymmetric tonic neck reflex.' Develop. Med. Child Neurol., 4, 363·
Lesny, I. (1960) 'The hypotonic forms of cerebral palsy.' Cerebral Palsy Bull., 2, 158.
Little Club, The (1959) Memorandum on terminology and classification of cerebral palsy. Cerebral Palsy Bull., 1, 27.
Magnus, R. (1926) 'Some results of studies in the physiology of posture.' Lancet. ii, 531-535, 585.
—— (1924) Korperstellung. Berlin: Springer.
Magoun, H. W., Rhines, R. (1946) 'Inhibitory mechanism in bulbar reticular formation.' J. Neurophysiol., 9, 165.
Mac Keith, R. (1964) 'The primary walking response and its facilitation by passive extension of the head.' Acta paediat. lat., 17, 710.
Milani-Comparetti, A. (1964) Paper given at the 4th International Study Group on Child Neurol. and Cerebral Palsy. Oxford.
Nathan, P. W. (1959) 'Intrathecal phenol to relieve spasticity in paraplegia.' Lancet, ii, 1099.
Peiper, A. (1961) Die Eigenart der Kindlichen Hirntaetigkeit. VEB, Leipzig: Thieme, pp. 155-294.
Phelps, W. M. (1941) 'The management of the cerebral palsied.' J. Amer. med. Ass. 117, 1621.
—— (1954) 'Cerebral palsy'. In Nelson's Textbook of Pediatrics. 6th ed. Philadelphia: Saunders. p. 1211.
Polani, P. E. (1959) 'The natural history of choreo-athetoid cerebral palsy.' Guys Hospital Rep., 32·
Prechtl, H., Beintema, D. (1964) The Neurological Examination of the Full-Term Newborn Infant. London: Spastics Soc./Heinemann. pp. 23, 45, 51, 55, 56.

Rademaker, G. C. J. (1935) Réactions Labyrinthiques et Equilibre. Paris: Masson.

Riddoch, G. Buzzard, E. F. (1921) 'Reflex movements and postural reactions in quadriplegia and hemiplegia with special reference to those of the upper limb.' *Brain*, **44**, 397.

Rushworth, G. (1960) 'Spasticity and rigidity. An experimental study and review.' *J. Neurol. Neurosurg. Psychiat.*, **23**, 99.

Schaltenbrand, G. (1927) 'The development of human motility and motor disturbances.' *Bull. N.Y. Acad. Med.*, **3**, 54.

—— (1925) 'Normale Bewegungs-und Lagereaktionen bei Kindern. *Dtsch. Z. Nervenheilk.* **87**, 23.

Sharrard, W. J. W. (1961) 'Danger of dislocation of the hip in asymmetrical spasticity of the thigh adductors.' *Cerebral Palsy Bull.*, **3**, 72.

Sherrington, C. S. (1913) 'Reflex inhibition as a factor in the co-ordination of movements and postures.' *Quart. J. exp. Physiol.* **6**, 251.

——, Mott, F. W. (1895) 'Experiments upon the influence of sensory nerves upon movements and nutrition of the limbs.' *Proc. roy. Soc.*, **57**, 431/38.

Tardieu, G. (1961) 'Danger of dislocation of the hip in asymmetrical spasticity of the thigh adductors.' *Cerebral Palsy Bull.*, **3**, 71.

Walshe, F. M. R. (1923) 'On certain tonic or postural reflexes in hemiplegia with special reference to the so-called associated movements.' *Brain*, **46**, 2.

—— (1921) 'On disorders of movement resulting from loss of postural tone, with special reference to the corpus striatum.' *Brain*, **44**, 539.

Weisz, S. (1938) 'Studies in equilibrium reactions.' *J. nerv. ment. Dis.*, **88**, 153.

Wilson, Kinnier, S. A. (1925) 'The Croonian Lectures on some disorders of motility and muscle tone with special reference to the corpus striatum.' *Lancet*, **ii**, 169.

Wilson, Kinnier, S. A., Walshe, F. M. R. (1914/15) 'The phenomenon of tonic innervation and its relation to motor apraxia.' *Brain*, **37**, 199.

Zador, J. (1938) Les Réactions d'Equilibre chez l'Homme. Paris: Masson.

Zappella, F. (1964) 'Postural reactions in 100 children with cerebral palsy and mental handicap.' *Develop. Med. Child Neurol.*, **6**, 475.

Zappella, C. M., Foley, F. (1964) 'The placing and supporting reactions in cerebral palsy.' *J. ment. Defic. Res.*, **8**, 17.

Clinics in Developmental Medicine

Now established as a wide-ranging and authoritative series on developmental medicine. Well produced, extensively illustrated, and reasonably priced. Books are published four times a year, and available singly or on a yearly subscription (£5, $15). Write for details to our distributors: William Heinemann Medical Books Ltd., The Press at Kingswood, Tadworth, Surrey, England.